THE

HISTORY OF ROME,

BY

TITUS LIVIUS.

BOOKS I. AND II.

LITERALLY TRANSLATED, WITH NOTES,

BY

D. SPILLAN, A.M., M.D.

WITH AN INTRODUCTION BY

EDWARD BROOKS, Jr.

PHILADELPHIA:

DAVID McKAY, PUBLISHER,

610 SOUTH WASHINGTON SQUARE

INTRODUCTION.

Titus Livius Patavinus was born at Patavium, now Padua, in 59 B.C. The records of his life are both meagre and unsatisfactory. His biographers have been compelled to rely almost entirely on Livy's own writings for facts concerning his life and in many instances have drawn largely on their imagination.

His family name Livius, it is thought was taken by one of his ancestors out of compliment to the great Livian gens at Rome and the surname Patavinus was doubtless added to distinguish the Livii at Patavium from those at Rome.

The early part of Livy's life was spent in his native town. At the time of his birth Patavium was a flourishing city comparing favorably with such large centres of industry as Alexandria and Gades. It is therefore quite probable that though Livy did not enjoy the educational advantages of his more fortunate contemporary Cicero, he nevertheless did not entirely lack the benefits to be derived from the association with and instruction

of intelligent and cultivated masters. This infer-
ence is strengthened by the fact that it is thought
his parents were wealthy and able to procure for
him every advantage which money could obtain.

The traditions relating to Patavium and its ancient connection with Rome are supposed to have
inspired Livy with a taste for history and there is
evidence in his writings that he prepared himself
for his great work by researches into the history
of his native town.

It was about the twenty-ninth year of his age
when he moved to Rome and took up his permanent residence there. Here his talents soon attracted the attention of the Emperor Augustus.
Though he enjoyed the personal friendship of the
emperor he does not, like many men of letters of
that period, appear to have been anything of a
courtier and he never took any part in political
life.

It is not known that he travelled extensively
but from his writings it appears that he at one
time paid a visit to Campania. It is said that he
was the tutor of Claudius who afterwards became
emperor and that he did much to stimulate his
historical zeal. This, however, is mere conjec-
ture.

Though taking no active part in politics, Livy
was nevertheless free to express his opinions on

the great political questions of the day. The traditions of the hard-won independence of his native
town doubtless influenced his sympathies in favor
of republican freedom and it is quite possible that
many of his utterances did not meet with the un-
qualified approval of Augustus. The latter, however, entertaining a sincere regard for the historian did not allow his friendship and patronage
to be affected by differences of opinion on political questions.

Having spent the greater part of his life in
Rome Livy retired to Padua during the reign of
Tiberius where he died in his sixty-seventh year.

The great achievement of Livy's life was his
History of the Roman People. This work which
the author modestly calls *Annales* (Annals) begins
with the landing of Æneas in Italy and traces
the development of the Roman state down to the
death of the commander Drusus in 9 B.C. It
originally consisted of one hundred and forty-two
books, of which only thirty-five are now extant,
viz.: Books I. to X. and XX. to XLV. The lost
books seem to have disappeared between the 7th
and 15th centuries. There is a story to the effect
that Pope Gregory I. burned all the copies of
Livy that could be found which is sometimes
offered as an explanation of the disappearance of
these books. This story, however, is said to rest

on no good evidence and it is probable that the loss was due to the difficulty of preserving such a voluminous work in days when the art of printing was unknown.

Although only about one-fourth of this great work is now extant, we are fortunate in having preserved to us short summaries of all the lost books except two. These summaries called *Epitomes*, while very meagre, give a fairly authentic description of the original work and have been ascribed to a Roman writer of the second century named Florus.

As a historian Livy has been the subject of considerable criticism on the ground of inaccuracy. It must be remembered, however, that he makes no pretensions to the character of a critical historian. In the preface of his work he states his purpose to be to perpetuate the achievements of the Roman people, "the lords of the world," and the main object of his writing was to erect a work which should be at once a lasting monument to the greatness of Rome and a warning to her citizens of the dangers which threatened them with destruction.

Livy's style represents the best period of Latin prose writers. His model was Cicero, and though perhaps in finish and rhythm he does not equal him, he nevertheless excels him in the formation

of his sentences and the adaptation of them to
his subject matter. His greatest fault is a tendency to use poetic diction in prose writing. This
fault was common to many prose writers of that
period, and it is greatly to Livy's credit that he
is less open to criticism in this respect than most
of his contemporaries.

The following pages contain a translation of
Books I. and II. of The History of Rome.

Book I. begins with the arrival of Æneas in
the territory of the Laurentines and his alliance
with their King Latinus, and relates the history
of the development of Rome down to the end of
the reign of Tarquin the Proud and the election
of the consuls Lucius Junius Brutus and Lucius
Tarquinius Collatinus.

Among the interesting traditions relating to the
early history of Rome, which this book mentions,
are the story of Romulus and Remus and the she-
wolf, the abduction of the Sabine women, the
cruel fate of Tarpeia who betrayed the Roman
citadel to the Sabines, the story of Numa Pompilius and the goddess Egeria, the celebrated triple
combat between the brothers Horatii and the
brothers Curatii, and the cruel and wicked inci-
dent of the reign of Tarquin the Proud.

Book II. commences with the consulship of
Brutus and Collatinus and continues the history

1 *

down to the time of the consulship of Æmilius and Fabius. Among the interesting events related in this book are the fatal combat between Brutus and Aruns, son of Tarquin, the heroic defence of the bridge across the Tiber by Horatius, the brave conduct of Mucius on the discovery of his attempt to assassinate Porsena, and the story of Coriolanus.

These events are related in a brief, but interesting, manner, and the reader cannot but feel himself well repaid after a perusal of the following pages.

THE HISTORY OF ROME.

BOOK I.

The coming of Æneas into Italy, and his achievements there; the
reign of Ascanius in Alba, and of the other Sylvian Kings. Romulus and Remus born. Amulius killed. Romulus builds Rome;
forms a Senate; makes war upon the Sabines; presents the *opima
spolia* to Jupiter Feretrius; divides the people into *curiæ;* his victo-
ries; is deified. Numa institutes the rites of religious worship;
builds a temple to Janus; and having made peace with all his
neighbors, closes it for the first time; enjoys a peaceful reign, and
is succeeded by Tullus Hostilius. War with the Albans; combat of
the Horatii and Curiatii. Alba demolished, and the Albans made
citizens of Rome. War declared against the Sabines: Tullus killed
by lightning. Ancus Marcius renews the religious institutions of
Numa; conquers the Latins; confers on them the right of citizenship, and assigns them the Aventine Hill to dwell on; adds the hill
Janiculum to the city; enlarges the bounds of the empire. In his
reign Lucumo comes to Rome; assumes the name of Tarquinius;
and, after the death of Ancus, is raised to the throne. He increases
the Senate, by adding to it a hundred new Senators; defeats the
Latins and Sabines; augments the centuries of knights; builds a wall
round the city; makes the common sewers; is slain by the sons of
Ancus after a reign of thirty-eight years; and is succeeded by Servius Tullius. He institutes the census; closes the lustrum, in which
eighty thousand citizens are said to have been enrolled; divides the
people into classes and centuries; enlarges the Pomœrium, and
adds the Quirinal, Viminal, and Esquiline hills to the city; after a
reign of forty years, is murdered by L. Tarquin, afterwards surnamed Superbus. He usurps the crown. Tarquin makes war on
the Volsci, and, with the plunder taken from them, builds a temple
to Jupiter Capitolinus. By a stratagem of his son, Sextus Tarquin,
he reduces the city of Gabii; after a reign of twenty-five years is de-
throned and banished, in consequence of the forcible violation of
the person of Lucretia by his son Sextus. L. Junius Brutus and L.
Tarquinius Collatinus first created consuls.

PREFACE.

WHETHER in tracing the history of the Roman people, from the foundation of the city, I shall employ myself to a useful purpose,[1] I am neither very certain, nor, if I were, dare I say: inasmuch as I observe, that it is both an old and hackneyed practice,[2] later authors always supposing that they will either adduce something more authentic in the facts, or, that they will excel the less polished ancients in their style of writing. Be that as it may, it will, at all events, be a satisfaction to me, that I too have contributed my share[3] to perpetuate the achievements of a people, the lords of the world; and if, amidst so great a number of historians,[4] my reputation should remain in obscurity, I may console myself with the celebrity and lustre of those who shall stand in the way of my fame. Moreover, the subject is both of immense labor, as being one which must be traced back for more than seven hundred years, and which, having set out from small beginnings, has increased to such a degree that it is now distressed by its own magnitude. And, to most readers, I doubt not but that the first origin and the events immediately succeeding, will afford but little pleas-

---

1 "Employ myself to a useful purpose"—*facere operæ pretium*, "to do a thing that is worth the trouble"—"to employ one's self to a good purpose."—See Scheller's "Lat. Lexicon."

2 "A practice"—*rem.*—Some, as Baker, refer it to *res populi R.* Others, as Stroth, to *res pop. Rom. perscribere.* ·

3 "My share"—*pro virili parte*, or, "to the best of my ability."

4 "Historians." Those mentioned by Livy himself are Q. Fabius Pictor, Valerius Antias, L. Piso, Q. Ælius Tubero, C. Licinius Macer, Cœlius, Polybius, etc.

ure, while they will be hastening to these later times,[1] in which the strength of this overgrown people has for a long period been working its own destruction. I, on the contrary, shall seek this, as a reward of my labor, viz., to withdraw myself from the view of the calamities, which our age has witnessed for so many years, so long as I am reviewing with my whole attention these ancient times, being free from every care[2] that may distract a writer's mind, though it can not warp it from the truth. The traditions which have come down to us of what happened before the building of the city, or before its building was contemplated, as being suitable rather to the fictions of poetry than to the genuine records of history, I have no intention either to affirm or refute. This indulgence is conceded to antiquity, that by blending things human with divine, it may make the origin of cities appear more venerable: and if any people might be allowed to consecrate their origin, and to ascribe it to the gods as its authors, such is the renown of the Roman people in war, that when they represent Mars, in particular, as their own parent and that of their founder, the nations of the world may submit to this as patiently as they submit to their sovereignty. But in whatever way these and such like matters shall be attended to, or judged of, I shall not deem of great importance. I would have every man apply his mind seriously to consider these points, viz., what their life and what their manners were; through what men and by what measures, both in peace and in war, their empire was

---

[1] "Hastening to these later times." The history of the recent civil wars would possess a more intense interest for the Romans of the Augustan age.

[2] "From every care." The fear of giving offense by expressing his opinions freely, and the sorrow which, as a patriot, he could not but feel in recording the civil wars of his countrymen.

acquired[1] and extended; then, as discipline gradually declined, let him follow in his thoughts their morals, at first
as slightly giving way, anon how they sunk more and more,
then began to fall headlong, until he reaches the present
times, when we can neither endure our vices, nor their
remedies. This it is which is particularly salutary and
profitable in the study of history, that you behold instances
of every variety of conduct displayed on a conspicuous
monument; that from thence you may select for yourself
and for your country that which you may imitate; thence
note what is shameful in the undertaking, and shameful in
the result, which you may avoid. But either a fond partiality for the task I have undertaken deceives me, or there
never was any state either greater, or more moral, or richer
in good examples, nor one into which luxury and avarice
made their entrance so late, and where poverty and fru-
gality were so much and so long honored; so that the less
wealth there was, the less desire was there. Of late, riches
have introduced avarice, and excessive pleasures a longing
for them, amidst luxury and a passion for ruining ourselves
and destroying every thing else. But let complaints, which
will not be agreeable even then, when perhaps they will be
also necessary, be kept aloof at least from the first stage of
commencing so great a work. We should rather, if it was
usual with us (historians) as it is with poets, begin with good
omens, vows, and prayers to the gods and goddesses to vouch-
safe good success to our efforts in so arduous an undertaking.

---

[1] "Acquired." This refers to the whole period antecedent to the
time when Ap. Claudius carried the Roman arms beyond Italy
against the Carthaginians; (2) *extended*, from that time till the fall of
Carthage; (3) *sinking*, the times of the Gracchi; (4) *gave way more and
more*, those of Sulla; (5) *precipitate*, those of Cæsar; (6) *the present times*,
those of Augustus after the battle of Actium.—*Stocker*.

CHAPTER I.

Now first of all it is sufficiently established that, Troy having been taken, the utmost severity was shown to all the other Trojans; but that towards two, Æneas and Antenor, the Greeks forbore all the rights of war, both in accordance with an ancient tie of hospitality, and because they had ever been the advisers of peace, and of the restoration of Helen—then that Antenor after various vicissitudes came into the innermost bay of the Adriatic Sea, with a body of the Heneti, who having been driven from Paphlagonia in consequence of a civil commotion, were in quest both of a settlement and a leader, their king, Pylæmenes, having been lost at Troy; and that the Heneti and Trojans, having expelled the Euganei, who dwelt between the sea and the Alps, took possession of the country; and the place where they first landed is called Troy; from whence also the name of Trojan is given to the canton; but the nation in general is called Veneti; that Æneas was driven from home by a similar calamity, but the fates leading him to the founding of a greater empire, he came first to Macedonia; that he sailed from thence to Sicily in quest of a settlement; that from Sicily he made for the Laurentine territory; this place also has the name of Troy. When the Trojans, having disembarked there, were driving plunder from the lands—as being persons to whom, after their almost immeasurable wandering, nothing was left but their arms and ships—Latinus the king, and the Aborigines, who then occupied those places, assembled in arms from the city and country to repel the violence of the new-comers. On this point the tradition is twofold: some say that Latinus, after being overcome in battle, made first a peace, and then an

alliance with Æneas : others that, when the armies were
drawn out in battle-array, before the signals were sounded,
Latinus advanced to the front of the troops and invited the
leader of the adventurers to a conference.   That he then
inquired who they were, whence (they had come), or by what
casualty they had left their home, and in quest of what
they had landed on the Laurentine territory : after he heard
that the host were Trojans, their chief Æneas, the son of
Anchises and Venus, and that, driven from their own country and their homes, which had been destroyed by fire, they
were seeking a settlement and a place for building a town,
struck with admiration of the noble origin of the nation and
of the hero, and their spirit, alike prepared for peace or
war, he confirmed the assurance of future friendship by giving his right hand ; that upon this a compact was struck between the chiefs, and mutual greetings passed between the
armies ; that Æneas was hospitably entertained by Latinus ;
that Latinus, in the presence of his household gods, added
a family league to the public one, by giving Æneas his
daughter in marriage.   This event confirms the Trojans in
the hope of at length terminating their wanderings by a
fixed and permanent settlement.   They build a town.   Æneas
calls it Lavinium, after the name of his wife.   In a short
time, too, a son was the issue of the new marriage, to whom
his parents gave the name of Ascanius.   ·

2. The Aborigines and Trojans were soon after attacked
together in war.   Turnus, king of the Rutulians, to whom
Lavinia had been affianced before the coming of Æneas,
enraged that a stranger had been preferred to himself, made
war on Æneas and Latinus together.   Neither side came off
from that contest with cause for rejoicing.   The Rutulians
were vanquished ; the victorious Aborigines and Trojans
lost their leader, Latinus.   Upon this Turnus and the Rutu-

lians, diffident of their strength, have recourse to the flourishing state of the Etruscans, and their king Mezentius; who, holding his court at Cœre, at that time an opulent town, being by no means pleased, even from the commencement, at the founding of the new city, and then considering that the Trojan power was increasing much more than was altogether consistent with the safety of the neighboring states, without reluctance joined his forces in alliance with the Rutulians. Æneas, in order to conciliate the minds of the Aborigines to meet the terror of so serious a war, called both nations Latins, so that they might all be not only under the same laws, but also the same name. Nor after that did the Aborigines yield to the Trojans in zeal and fidelity towards their king Æneas; relying, therefore, on this disposition of the two nations, who were now daily coalescing more and more, although Etruria was so powerful that it filled with the fame of its prowess not only the land but the sea also, through the whole length of Italy, from the Alps to the Sicilian Strait, though he might have repelled the war by means of fortifications, yet he led out his forces to the field. Upon this a battle ensued successful to the Latins, the last also of the mortal acts of Æneas. He was buried, by whatever name human and divine laws require him to be called,[1] on the banks of the River Numicius. They call him Jupiter Indiges.

3. Ascanius, the son of Æneas, was not yet old enough to take the government upon him; that government, however, remained secure for him till the age of maturity. In the interim, the Latin state and the kingdom of his grandfather

---

[1] Æneas, being now deified, could not be called by his human name; and in speaking of his being buried, it would be improper to name him by his divine title.—*Indigetem.* He is called by Dionysius χθόνιος θεός.

and father was secured for the boy under the regency of his mother (such capacity was there in Lavinia). I have some doubts (for who can state as certain a matter of such antiquity) whether this was the Ascanius, or one older than he, born of Creusa before the fall of Troy, and the companion of his father in his flight from thence, the same whom, being called Iulus, the Julian family called the author of their name. This Ascanius, wheresoever and of whatever mother born (it is at least certain that he was the son of Æneas), Lavinium being overstocked with inhabitants, left that flourishing and, considering these times, wealthy city to his mother or stepmother, and built for himself a new one at the foot of Mount Alba, which, being extended on the ridge of a hill, was, from its situation, called Longa Alba. Between the founding of Lavinium and the transplanting this colony to Longa Alba about thirty years intervened. Yet its power had increased to such a degree, especially after the defeat of the Etrurians, that not even upon the death of Æneas, nor after that, during the regency of Lavinia, and the first essays of the young prince's reign, did Mezentius, the Etrurians, or any other of its neighbors dare to take up arms against it. A peace had been concluded between the two nations on these terms, that the River Albula, now called Tiber, should be the common boundary between the Etrurians and Latins. After him Sylvius, the son of Ascanius, born by some accident in a wood, ascends the throne. He was the father of Æneas Sylvius, who afterwards begot Latinus Sylvius. By him several colonies called the ancient Latins, were transplanted. From this time, all the princes who reigned at Alba had the surname of Sylvius. From Latinus sprung Alba; from Alba, Atys; from Atys, Capys; from Capys, Capetus; from Capetus, Tiberinus, who, being drowned in crossing the River Albula,

gave it a name famous with posterity.   Then Agrippa, the
son of Tiberinus; after Agrippa, Romulus Silvius ascends
the throne, in succession to his father.   The latter, having
been killed by a thunder-bolt, left the kingdom to Aventinus,
who being buried on that hill, which is now part of the city
of Rome, gave his name to it.   After him reigns Pioca; he
begets Numitor and Amulius.   To Numitor, his eldest son,
he bequeaths the ancient kingdom of the Sylvian family.
But force prevailed more than the father's will or the respect due to seniority : for Amulius, having expelled his
brother, seizes the kingdom ; he adds crime to crime, murders his brother's male issue ; and under pretense of doing
his brother's daughter, Rhea Sylvia, honor, having made
her a vestal virgin, by obliging her to perpetual virginity,
he deprives her of all hopes of issue.

4. But, in my opinion, the origin of so great a city, and
the establishment of an empire next in power to that of the
gods, was due to the Fates.   The vestal Rhea, being de-
flowered by force, when she had brought forth twins, declares
Mars to be the father of her illegitimate offspring, either
because she believed it to be so, or because a god was a more
creditable author of her offense.   But neither gods nor men
protect her or her children from the king's cruelty ; the
priestess is bound and thrown into prison ; the children he
commands to be thrown into the current of the river.   By
some interposition of providence,[1] the Tiber having over-
flowed its banks in stagnant pools, did not admit of any access to the regular bed of the river; and the bearers supposed that the infants could be drowned in water however
still ; thus, as if they had effectually executed the king's
orders, they expose the boys in the nearest land-flood, where

---

[1] *Forte quàdam divinitus.* Θείᾳτινι τύχη. Plut.

now stands the ficus Ruminalis (they say that it was called Romularis). The country thereabout was then a vast wilderness. The tradition is, that when the water, subsiding, had left the floating trough, in which the children had been exposed, on dry ground, a thirsty she-wolf, coming from the neighboring mountains, directed her course to the cries of the infants, and that she held down her dugs to them with so much gentleness, that the keeper of the king's flock found her licking the boys with her tongue. It is said his name was Faustulus; and that they were carried by him to his homestead to be nursed by his wife Laurentia. Some are of opinion that she was called Lupa among the shepherds, from her being a common prostitute, and that this gave rise to the surprising story. The children thus born, and thus brought up, when arrived at the years of manhood, did not loiter away their time in tending the folds or following the flocks, but roamed and hunted in the forests. Having by this exercise improved their strength and courage, they not only encountered wild beasts, but even attacked robbers laden with plunder, and afterwards divided the spoil among the shepherds. And in company with these, the number of their young associates daily increasing, they carried on their business and their sports.

5. They say that the festival of the lupercal, as now celebrated, was even at that time solemnized on the Palatine hill, which, from Palanteum, a city of Arcadia, was first called Palatium, and afterwards Mount Palatine. There they say that Evander, who belonged to the tribe of Arcadians,[1] that for many years before had possessed that country, appointed the observance of a feast, introduced from Arcadia, in such manner, that young men ran about

---

[1] Scil, " The Pallantean."

naked in sport and wantonness, doing honor to Pan Ly-
cæus, whom the Romans afterwards called Inuus.   That the
robbers, through rage at the loss of their booty, having
lain in wait for them while intent on this sport, as the
festival was now well known, while Romulus vigorously
defended himself, took Remus prisoner; that they delivered him up, when taken, to King Amulius, accusing him
with the utmost effrontery.   They principally alleged it as
a charge against them, that they had made incursions
upon Numitor's lands, and plundered them in a hostile
manner, having assembled a band of young men for the
purpose.   Upon this, Remus was delivered to Numitor to
be punished.   Now, from the very first, Faustulus had entertained hopes that the boys whom he was bringing up were
of the blood royal; for he both knew that the children
had been exposed by the king's orders, and that the time
at which he had taken them up agreed exactly with that
period; but he had been unwilling that the matter, as not
being yet ripe for discovery, should be disclosed till either
a fit opportunity or necessity should arise.   Necessity came
first; accordingly, impelled by fear, he discovers the whole
affair to Romulus.   By accident also, while he had Remus
in custody, and had heard that the brothers were twins, on
comparing their age, and *observing* their turn of mind entirely
free from servility, the recollection of his grandchildren
struck Numitor; and on making inquiries[1] he arrived at
the same conclusion, so that he was well nigh recognizing
Remus.   Thus a plot is concerted for the king on all sides.
Romulus, not accompanied by a body of young men (for
he was unequal to open force), but having commanded the

---

[1] By all his inquiries he arrived at the same conclusion as before,
viz., that they were his grandchildren.

shepherds to come to the palace by different roads at a fixed time, forces his way to the king; and Remus, with another party from Numitor's house, assists his brother, and so they kill the king.

6. Numitor, at the beginning of the fray, having given out that enemies had invaded the city, and assaulted the palace, after he had drawn off the Alban youth to secure the citadel with a garrison and arms, when he saw the young men, after they had killed the king, advancing to congratulate him, immediately called an assembly of the people, and represented to them the unnatural behavior of his brother towards him, the extraction of his grand-children, the manner of their birth and education, and how they came to be discovered; then he informed them of the king's death, and that he was killed by his orders. When the young princes, coming up with their band through the middle of the assembly, saluted their grandfather king, an approving shout, following from all the people present, ratified to him both that title and the sovereignty. Thus the government of Alba being committed to Numitor, a desire seized Romulus and Remus to build a city on the spot where they had been exposed and brought up. And there was an overflowing population of Albans and of Latins. The shepherds too had come into that design, and all these readily inspired hopes that Alba and Lavinium would be but petty places in comparison with the city which they intended to build. But ambition of the sovereignty, the bane of their grandfather, interrupted these designs, and thence arose a shameful quarrel from a beginning sufficiently amicable. For as they were twins, and the respect due to seniority could not determine the point, they agreed to leave to the tutelary gods of the place to choose by augury which should give a name to the new city, which govern it when built.

7. Romulus chose the Palatine and Remus the Aventine hill as their stands to make their observations. It is said, that to Remus an omen came first, six vultures; and now, the omen having been declared, when double the number presented itself to Romulus, his own party saluted each king; the former claimed the kingdom on the ground of priority of time, the latter on account of the number of birds. Upon this, having met in an altercation, from the contest of angry feelings they turn to bloodshed; there Remus fell from a blow received in the crowd. A more common account is, that Remus in derision of his brother, leaped over his new-built wall, and was for that reason, slain by Romulus in a passion; who after sharply chiding him, added words to this effect: "So shall every one fare who shall dare to leap over my fortifications."[1] Thus Romulus got the sovereignty to himself; the city, when built, was called after the name of its founder. His first work was to fortify the Palatine hill, where he had been educated. To the other gods he offers sacrifices according to the Alban rite; to Hercules, according to the Grecian rite, as they had been instituted by Evander. There is a tradition that Hercules, having killed Geryon, drove his oxen, which were extremely beautiful, into those places; and that, after swimming over the Tiber, and driving the cattle before him, being fatigued with travelling, he laid himself down on the banks of the river, in a grassy place, to refresh them with rest and rich pasture. When sleep had overpowered him, satiated with food and wine, a shepherd of the place, named Cacus, presuming on his strength, and charmed with the beauty of the oxen, wished to pur-

[1] According to Cato, Rome was founded on the day of the *Palilia*, the 11th of the Calends of May, in the first year of the 7th Olympiad, and 751 B.C. This is two years short of Varro's computation.

loin that booty, but because, if he had driven them forward into the cave, their footsteps would have guided the
search of their owner thither, he therefore drew the most
beautiful of them, one by one, by the tails, backward into
a cave. Hercules, awaking at daybreak, when he had sur-
veyed his herd, and observed that some of them were missing, goes directly to the nearest cave, to see if by chance
their footsteps would lead him thither. But when he observed that they were all turned from it, and directed him
no other way, confounded, and not knowing what to do, he
began to drive his cattle out of that unlucky place. Upon
this, some of the cows, as they usually do, lowed on missing
those that were left; and the lowing of those that were confined being returned from the cave, made Hercules turn
that way. And when Cacus attempted to prevent him by
force, as he was proceeding to the cave, being struck with a
club he was slain, vainly imploring the assistance of the
shepherds. At that time Evander, who had fled from the
Peloponnesus, ruled this country more by his credit and
reputation than absolute sway. He was a person highly revered for his wondrous knowledge of letters,[1] a discovery
that was entirely new and surprising to men ignorant of
every art; but more highly respected on account of the
supposed divinity of his mother Carmenta, whom the nations had admired as a prophetess, before the coming of the
Sybil into Italy. This prince, alarmed by the concourse of
the shepherds, hastily crowding around the stranger, whom
they charged with open murder, after he heard the act and
the cause of the act, observing the person and mien of the
hero to be larger, and his gait more majestic than human,
asked who he was? As soon as he was informed of his

---

[1] He taught the Italians to read and write.

name, his father, and his native country, he said, "Hail! Hercules! son of Jupiter, my mother, a truth-telling interpreter of the gods, has revealed to me that thou shalt increase the number of the celestials; and that to thee an altar shall be dedicated here, which some ages hence the most powerful people on earth shall call Ara Maxima, and honor according to thy own institution." Hercules, having given him his right hand, said, "That he accepted the omen, and would fulfil the predictions of the fates, by building and consecrating an altar." There for the first time a sacrifice was offered to Hercules of a chosen heifer, taken from the herd, the Potitii and Pinarii, who were then the most distinguished families that inhabited these parts, having been invited to the service and the entertainment. It so happened that the Potitii were present in due time, and the entrails were set before them; when they were eaten up, the Pinarii came to the remainder of the feast. From this time it was ordained, that while the Pinarian family subsisted, none of them should eat of the entrails of the solemn sacrifices. The Potitii, being instructed by Evander, discharged this sacred function as priests for many ages, until the office solemnly appropriated to their family, being delegated to public slaves, their whole race became extinct. This was the only foreign religious institution which Romulus adopted, being even then an abettor of immortality attained by merit, to which his own destinies were conducting him.

8. The duties of religion having been duly performed, and the multitude summoned to a meeting, as they could be incorporated into one people by no other means than fixed rules, he gave them a code of laws, and judging that these would be best respected by this rude class of men, if he made himself dignified by the insignia of authority, he assumed a more majestic appearance both in his other ap-

2

pointments, and especially by taking twelve lictors to attend
him.   Some think that he chose this number of officers from
that of the birds, which in the augury had portended the
kingdom to him.   I do not object to be of the opinion of
those who will have it that the apparitors (in general), and
this particular class of them,[1] and even their number, was·
taken from their neighbors the Etrurians, from whom were
borrowed the curule chair, and the gown edged with purple ;
and that the Etrurians adopted that number because their
king, being elected in common from twelve states, each state
assigned him one lictor.   Meanwhile the city increased by
their taking in various lots of ground for buildings, while
they built rather with a view to future numbers than for the
population[2] which they then had.   Then, lest the size of
the city might be of no avail, in order to augment the population, according to the ancient policy of the founders of
cities, who, after drawing together to them an obscure and
mean multitude, used to feign that their offspring sprung
out of the earth, he opened as a sanctuary, a place which is
now inclosed as you go down "to the two groves."[3]   Hither
fled from the neighboring states, without distinction, whether freemen or slaves, crowds of all sorts, desirous of
change; and this was the first accession of strength to their
rising greatness.   When he was now not dissatisfied with

[1] *Apparitores hoc genus.*   There is something incorrect in the language of the original here.   In my version I have followed Drakenborch.   Walker, in his edition, proposes to read *ut* for *et :* thus, *Quibus
ut apparitores et hoc genus ab Etruscis—numerum quoque ipsum ductum
placet,* "*Who will have it, that as public servants of this kind, so was their
number also derived from the Etrurians.*"

[2] The population at that time consisted of not more than 3000 foot,
and less than 300 horse.   At the death of Romulus it is said to have
amounted to 46,000 foot and almost 1000 horse.

[3] τὸ μεταξὺ χωρίον τοῦ τε Καπιτωλίου καὶ τῆς ἄκρας ὃ καλεῖται νῦν κατὰ
τὴν Ῥωμαίων διάλεκτον μεθόριον δυοῖν δρυμῶν.   Dio. ii. 15.

his strength, he next sets about forming some means of directing that strength. He creates one hundred Senators, either because that number was sufficient, or because there were only one hundred who could name their fathers. They certainly were called Fathers through respect, and their descendants Patricians.

9. And now the Roman state was become so powerful, that it was a match for any of the neighboring nations in war, but, from the paucity of women, its greatness could only last for one age of man; for they had no hope of issue at home, nor had they any intermarriages with their neighbors. Therefore, by the advice of the Fathers, Romulus sent ambassadors to the neighboring states to solicit an alliance and the privilege of intermarriage for his new subjects. "That cities, like everything else, rose from very humble beginnings. That those which the gods and their own merit aided, gained great power and high renown. That he knew full well, both that the gods had aided the origin of Rome, and that merit would not be wanting. Wherefore that, as men, they should feel no reluctance to mix their blood and race with men." Nowhere did the embassy obtain a favorable hearing: so much did they at the same time despise, and dread for themselves and their posterity, so great a power growing up in the midst of them. They were dismissed by the greater part with the repeated question, "Whether they had opened any asylum for women also, for that such a plan only could obtain them suitable matches?" The Roman youth resented this conduct bitterly, and the matter unquestionably began to point towards violence. Romulus, in order that he might afford a favorable time and place for this, dissembling his resentment, purposely [1] prepares games in honor of Neptunis Equestris;

---

[1] *Ex industria—dedita—operā—ἀπὸ παρασκευῆς.*

he calls them Consualia. He then orders the spectacle to
be proclaimed among their neighbors; and they prepare for
the celebration with all the magnificence they were then
acquainted with or were capable of doing, that they might
render the matter famous, and an object of expectation.
Great numbers assembled, from a desire also of seeing the
new city; especially their nearest neighbors, the Cæninenses, Crustumini, and Antemnates.   Moreover the whole multitude of the Sabines came, with their wives and ·children.
Having been hospitably invited to the different houses,
when they had seen the situation, and fortifications, and the
city crowded with houses, they became astonished that the
Roman power had increased so rapidly.   When the time of
the spectacle came on, and while their minds and eyes were
intent upon it, according to concert a tumult began, and
upon a signal given the Roman youth ran different ways to
carry off the virgins by force. A great number were carried off at hap-hazard, according as they fell into their
hands. Persons from the common people, who had been
charged with the task, conveyed to their houses some women
of surpassing beauty, destined for the leading Senators.
They say that one, far distinguished beyond the others for
stature and beauty, was carried off by the party of one Tha-
lassius, and while many inquired to whom they were carrying her, they cried out every now and then, in order that
no one might molest her, that she was being taken to Tha-
lassius; that from this circumstance this term became a
nuptial one. The festival being disturbed by this alarm,
the parents of the young women retire in grief, appealing
to the compact of violated hospitality, and invoking the
god to whose festival and games they had come, deceived by
the pretense of religion and good faith. Neither had the
ravished virgins better hopes of their condition, or less in-

dignation. But Romulus in person went about and declared, "That what was done was owing to the pride of their fathers, who had refused to grant the privilege of marriage to their neighbors; but notwithstanding, they should be joined in lawful wedlock, participate in all their possessions and civil privileges, and, than which nothing can be dearer to the human heart, in their common children. He begged them only to assuage the fierceness of their anger, and cheerfully surrender their affections to those to whom fortune had consigned their persons." [He added] "That from injuries love and friendship often arise; and that they should find them kinder husbands on this account, because each of them, besides the performance of his conjugal duty, would endeavor to the utmost of his power to make up for the want of their parents and native country." To this the caresses of the husbands were added, excusing what they had done on the plea of passion and love, arguments that work most successfully on women's hearts.

10. The minds of the ravished virgins were soon much soothed, but their parents, by putting on mourning, and tears and complaints, roused the states. Nor did they confine their resentment to their own homes, but they flocked from all quarters to Titus Tatius, king of the Sabines; and because he bore the greatest character in these parts, embassies were sent to him. The Cæninenses, Crustumini, and Antemnates were people to whom a considerable portion of the outrage extended. To them Tatius and the Sabines seemed to proceed somewhat dilatorily. Nor even do the Crustumini and Antemnates bestir themselves with sufficient activity to suit the impatience and rage of the Cæninenses. Accordingly the state of the Cæninenses by itself makes an irruption into the Roman territory. But Romulus with his army met them ravaging the country in straggling parties,

and by a slight engagement convinces them that resentment without strength is of no avail. He defeats and routs their army, pursues it when routed, kills and despoils their king in battle, and, having slain their general, takes the city at the first assault. From thence, having led back his victorious army, and being a man highly distinguished by his · exploits, and one who could place them in the best light, went in state to the capitol, carrying before him, suspended on a frame curiously wrought for that purpose, the spoils of the enemy's general, whom he had slain, and there, after he had laid them down at the foot of an oak held sacred by the shepherds, together with the offering, he marked out the bounds for a temple of Jupiter, and gave a surname to the god: "Jupiter Feretrius," he says, "I, king Romulus, upon my victory, present to thee these royal arms, and to thee I dedicate a temple within those regions which I have now marked out in my mind, as a receptacle for the grand spoils, which my successors, following my example, shall, upon their killing the kings or generals of the enemy, offer to thee." This is the origin of that temple, the first consecrated at Rome. It afterwards so pleased the gods both that the declaration of the founder of the temple should not be frustrated by which he announced that his posterity should offer such spoils, and that the glory of that offering should not be depreciated by the great number of those who shared it. During so many years, and amidst so many wars since that time, grand spoils have been only twice gained,[1] so rare has been the successful attainment of that honor.

11. While the Romans are achieving these exploits, the army of the Antemnates, taking advantage of their ab-

---

[1] Two: one by A. Cornelius Cossus for slaying L. Tolumnius, king of Veii, u. c. 318; another by M. Claudius Marcellus, for killing Viridomarus, king of the Gauls, u. c. 532.

sence, makes an incursion into the Roman territories in a hostile manner. A Roman legion being marched out in haste against these also, surprise them while straggling through the fields. Accordingly the enemy were routed at the very first shout and charge : their town taken ; and as Romulus was returning, exulting for this double victory, his consort, Hersilia, importuned by the entreaties of the captured women, beseeches him "to pardon their fathers, and to admit them to the privilege of citizens ; that thus his power might be strengthened by a reconciliation." Her request was readily granted. After this he marched against the Crustumini, who were commencing hostilities ; but as their spirits were sunk by the defeat of their neighbors, there was still less resistance there. Colonies were sent to both places, but more were found to give in their names for Crustuminum, because of the fertility of the soil. Migrations in great numbers were also made from thence to Rome, chiefly by the parents and relatives of the ravished women. The last war broke out on the part of the Sabines, and proved by far the most formidable : for they did nothing through anger or cupidity ; nor did they make a show of war before they actually began it. To prudence stratagem also was added. Sp. Tarpeius commanded the Roman citadel ; Tatius bribes his maiden daughter with gold, to admit armed soldiers into the citadel : she had gone by chance outside the walls to fetch water for the sacrifice. Those who were admitted crushed her to death by heaping their arms upon her ; either that the citadel might seem rather to have been taken by storm, or for the purpose of establishing a precedent that no faith should, under any circumstances, be kept with a traitor. A story is added, that the Sabines commonly wore on their left arm golden bracelets of great weight, and large rings set with precious stones, and that she bargained with them for what they had on their left hands; hence that their shields were thrown upon her instead of the golden presents. There are some who say that in pursuance of the compact to deliver up what was on their left hands, she expressly demanded their shields, and that appearing to act with treachery, she was killed by the reward of her own choosing.

12. The Sabines, however, kept possession of the citadel: and on the day after, when the Roman army, drawn up in order of battle, filled up all the ground lying between the Palatine and Capitoline hills, they did not descend from thence into the plain till the Romans, fired with resentment, and with a desire of retaking the citadel, advanced to attack them. Two chiefs, one on each side, animated the battle, viz., Mettus Curtius on the part of the Sabines, Hostus Hostilius on that of the Romans. The latter, in the front ranks, supported the Roman cause by his courage and bravery, on disadvantageous ground. As soon as Hostus fell, the Roman line immediately gave way, and was beaten to the old gate of the Palatium. Romulus, himself too carried away with the general rout, raising his arms to heaven, says: "O Jupiter, commanded by thy birds, I here laid the first foundation of the city on the Palatine hill. The Sabines are in possession of the citadel, purchased by fraud. From thence they are now advancing hither, sword in hand, having already passed the middle of the valley. But do thou, father of gods and men, keep back the enemy at least from hence, dispel the terror of the Romans, and stop their shameful flight. Here I solemnly vow to build a temple to thee as Jupiter Stator, as a monument to posterity that this city was saved by thy immediate aid." Having offered up this prayer, as if he had felt that his prayers were heard, he cries out, "At this spot, Romans, Jupiter, supremely

good and great, commands you to halt, and renew the
fight." The Romans halted as if they had been commanded
by a voice from heaven; Romulus himself flies to the foremost ranks. Mettus Curtius, on the part of the Sabines, had
rushed down at the head of his army from the citadel, and
driven the Romans in disorder over the whole ground now
occupied by the Forum. He was already not far from the
gate of the Palatium, crying out, "We have defeated these
perfidious strangers, these dastardly enemies. They now
feel that it is one thing to ravish virgins, another far different to fight with men." On him, thus vaunting, Romulus makes an attack with a band of the most courageous
youths. It happened that Mettus was then fighting on
horseback; he was on that account the more easily repulsed: the Romans pursue him when repulsed: and the
rest of the Roman army, encouraged by the gallant behavior of their king, routs the Sabines. Mettus, his horse
taking fright at the din of his pursuers, threw himself into
a lake; and this circumstance drew the attention of the
Sabines at the risk of so important a person. He, however,
his own party beckoning and calling to him, acquires new
courage from the affection of his many friends, and makes
his escape. The Romans and Sabines renew the battle in
the valley between the hills; but Roman prowess had the
advantage.

13. At this juncture the Sabine women, from the outrage on whom the war originated, with hair dishevelled
and garments rent, the timidity of their sex being overcome by such dreadful scenes, had the courage to throw
themselves amidst the flying weapons, and making a rush
across, to part the incensed armies and assuage their fury;
imploring their fathers on the one side, their husbands on
the other, "that as fathers-in-law and sons-in-law they

2 *

would not contaminate each other with impious blood, nor
stain their offspring with parricide, the one their grand-
children, the other their children.[1] If you are dissatisfied
with the affinity between you, if with our marriages, turn
your resentment against us ; we are the cause of war, we of
wounds and of bloodshed to our husbands and parents. It
were better that we perish than live widowed or fatherless
without one or other of you." The circumstance affects
both the multitude and the leaders. Silence and a sudden
suspension ensue. Upon this the leaders come forward in
order to concert a treaty, and they not only conclude a peace,
but form one state out of two. They associate the regal
power, and transfer the entire sovereignty to Rome. The
city being thus doubled, that some compliment might be
paid to the Sabines, they were called Quirites, from Cures.
As a memorial of this battle, they called the place where
the horse, after getting out of the deep marsh, first set Curtius in shallow water, the Curtian Lake. This happy peace
following suddenly a war so distressing, rendered the Sabine
women still dearer to their husbands and parents, and above
all to Romulus himself. Accordingly, when he divided the
people into thirty curiæ, he called the curiæ by their names.
Since, without doubt, the number of the Sabine women was
considerably greater than this, it is not recorded whether
those who were to give their names to the curiæ were selected
on account of their age, or their own or their husbands'
rank, or by lot. At the same time three centuries of
knights were enrolled, called Ramnenses, from Romulus ;
Tatienses, from Titus Tatius. The reason of the name and
origin of the Luceres is uncertain.

---

[1] *Nepotum et liberûm progeniem* — Nepotes et liberos—υἱες 'Αχαιωνοὶ
'Αχαιοι.

14. Thenceforward the two kings held the regal power not only in common, but in concord also. Several years after, some relatives of King Tatius beat the ambassadors of the Laurentes, and when the Laurentes commenced proceedings according to the law of nations, the influence of his friends and their importunities had more weight with Tatius. He therefore drew upon himself the punishment due to them; for he is slain at Lavinium in a tumult which arose on his going thither to an anniversary sacrifice. They say that Romulus resented this with less severity than the case required, either by reason of their association in the kingly power being devoid of cordiality, or because he believed that he was justly killed. He therefore declined going to war; in order, however, that the ill-treatment of the ambassadors and the murder of the king might be expiated, the treaty was renewed between the cities of Rome and Lavinium. With this party, indeed, peace continued, contrary to expectation; another war broke out much nearer home, and almost at the very gates. The Fidenates, thinking that a power too near to themselves was growing to a height, resolve to make war, before their strength should become as great as it was apparent it would be. An armed body of young men being sent in, all the land is laid waste between the city and Fidenæ. Then turning to the left, because the Tiber confined them on the right, they continue their depredations to the great consternation of the peasantry. The sudden alarm reaching the city from the country, served as the first announcement. Romulus, roused at this circumstance (for a war so near home could not admit of delay), leads out his army; he pitches his camp a mile from Fidenæ. Having left there a small garrison, marching out with all his forces, he commanded a party of his soldiers to lie in ambush in a place hidden by thick bushes

which were planted around.[1] Then advancing with the
greater part of the foot and all the horse, and riding up to
the very gates of the city in a disorderly and menacing manner, he drew out the enemy, the very thing he wanted.
The same mode of fighting on the part of the cavalry likewise made the cause of the flight, which was to be counterfeited, appear less surprising ; and when, the horse seeming
irresolute, as if in deliberation whether to fight or fly, the
infantry also retreated, the enemy suddenly rushed from the
crowded gates, after they had made an impression on the
Roman line, are drawn on to the place of ambuscade in their
eagerness to press on and pursue. Upon this the Romans,
rising suddenly, attack the enemy's line in flank. The
standards of those who had been left behind on guard,
advancing from the camp, further increase the panic.
The Fidenates, thus dismayed with terrors from so many
quarters, turn their backs almost before Romulus and those
who had accompanied him on horseback could wheel their
horses round ; and those who a little before had pursued
men pretending to fly, now ran back to the town in much
greater disorder, for their flight was in earnest. They did
not, however, get clear of the enemy : the Romans pressing
on their rear rush in, as it were, in one body before the
gates could be shut against them.

15. The minds of the Veientes being excited by the con-
tagious influence of the Fidenatian war, both from the tie of
consanguinity, for the Fidenates also were Etrurians, and
because the very proximity of situation, in case the Roman
arms should be turned against all their neighbors, urged
them on, they made an incursion on the Roman territories,
more to commit depredations than after the manner of a

---

[1] The original has undergone various changes here : my version
coincides with the reading, *locis circâ densa obsita virgulta obscuris.*

regular war. Accordingly, without pitching a camp, or
awaiting the approach of the enemy's army, they returned
to Veii, carrying with them the booty collected from the
lands; the Roman army on the other side, when they did
not find the enemy in the country, being prepared for and
determined on a decisive action, cross the Tiber. And when
the Veientes heard that they were pitching a camp, and intended to advance to the city, they came out to meet them,
that they might rather decide the matter in the open field,
than be shut up and fight from their houses and walls.
Here the Roman king obtained the victory, his power not
being aided by any stratagem, merely by the strength of his
veteran army; and having pursued the routed enemies to
their walls, he made no attempt on the city, strong as it was
by its fortifications, and well defended by its situation; on
his return he lays waste their lands, rather from a desire of
revenge than booty. And the Veientes, being humbled by
that loss no less than by the unsuccessful battle, send ambassadors to Rome to sue for peace. A truce for one hundred
years was granted them after they were fined a part of their
land. These are the principal transactions which occurred
during the reign of Romulus, in peace and war, none of
which seem inconsistent with the belief of his divine original, or of the deification attributed to him after death,
neither his spirit in recovering his grandfather's kingdom,
nor his project of building a city, nor that of strengthening
it by the arts of war and peace. For by the strength attained from that outset under him, it became so powerful,
that for forty years after it enjoyed a profound peace. He
was, however, dearer to the people than to the fathers; but
above all others he was most beloved by the soldiers. And
he kept three hundred of them armed as a body-guard not
only in war but in peace, whom he called Celeres.

16. After performing these immortal achievements, while he was holding an assembly of the people for reviewing his army, in the plain near the Lake of Capra, on a sudden a storm having arisen, with great thunder and lightning, enveloped the king in so dense a mist that it took all sight of him from the assembly. Nor was Romulus after this seen on earth. The consternation being at length over, and fine clear weather succeeding so turbulent a day, when the Roman youth saw the royal seat empty, though they readily believed the fathers who had stood nearest him, that he was carried aloft by the storm, yet, struck with the dread, as it were of orphanage, they preserved a sorrowful silence for a considerable time. Then, a commencement having been made by a few, the whole multitude salute Romulus a god, son of a god, the king and parent of the Roman city; they implore his favor with prayers, that he would be pleased always propitiously to preserve his own offspring. I believe that even then there were some who silently surmised that the king had been torn in pieces by the hands of the fathers; for this rumor also spread, but was not credited; their admiration of the man, and the consternation felt at the moment, attached importance to the other report. By the contrivance also of one individual, additional credit is said to have been gained to the matter. For Proculus Julius, while the state was still troubled with regret for the king, and felt incensed against the Senators—a person of weight, as we are told, in any matter however important—comes forward to the assembly: "Romans," he says, "Romulus, the father of this city, suddenly descending from heaven, appeared to me this day at daybreak. While I stood covered with awe, and filled with a religious dread, beseeching him to allow me to see him face to face, he said, Go tell the Romans that the gods so will that my Rome should be-

come the capital of the world.   Therefore let them cultivate
the art of war, and let them know and hand down to posterity, that no human power shall be able to withstand the
Roman arms. Having said this, he ascended up to heaven."
It is surprising what credit was given to the man on his
making this announcement, and how much the regret of the
common people and army for the loss of Romulus was assuaged upon the assurance of his immortality.

17. Meanwhile ambition and contention for the throne
actuated the minds of the fathers ; factions had not yet
sprung up from individuals, because, among a new people,
no one person was eminently distinguished above the rest :
the contest was carried on between the different orders.
The descendants of the Sabines wished a king to be elected
out of their body, lest, because there had been no king on
their side since the death of Tatius, they might lose their
claim to the crown[1] according to the compact of equal participation.   The old Romans spurned the idea of a foreign
prince.   Amidst this diversity of views, however, all were
anxious that there should be a king, they not having yet
tasted the sweets of liberty.   Fear then seized the Senators,
lest the minds of the surrounding states being incensed
against them, some foreign power should attack the state,
now without a government, and the army without a leader.
It was therefore their wish that there should be some head,
but no one could bring himself to give way to another.
Thus the hundred Senators divide the government among
them, ten decuries being formed, and one selected from
each decury, who was to have the chief direction of affairs.
Ten governed ; one only was attended with the insignia of
authority and the lictors ; their power was limited to the

---

[1] Although, according to the terms of the alliance, the Sabines
and the Romans were to be in all respects on an equal footing.

space of five days, and it passed through all in rotation, and the interval between a kingly government lasted a year. From the circumstance it was called an Interregnum, a term which holds good even now. But the people began to murmur that their slavery was multiplied, and that they had got a hundred sovereigns instead of one, and they seemed determined to bear no authority but that of a king, and that one of their own choosing. When the fathers perceived that such schemes were in agitation, thinking it advisable to offer them, of their own accord, what they were sure to lose; they thus conciliate the favor of the people by yielding to them the supreme power, yet in such a manner as to grant them no greater privilege than they reserved to themselves. For they decreed that, when the people should choose a king, the election should be valid, if the Senate approved. And the same forms[1] are observed at this day in passing laws and electing magistrates, though their efficacy has been taken away; for, before the people begin to vote, the Senators declare their approbation, while the result of the elections is still uncertain. Then the interrex, having called an assembly of the people, addressed them in this manner: "Do you, Romans, choose yourself a king, and may it prove fortunate, happy, and auspicious to you; so the fathers have determined. Then, if you choose a prince worthy to succeed Romulus, the fathers will confirm your choice." This concession was so pleasing to the people that not to be outdone in generosity, they only voted, and required that the Senate should determine who should be king of Rome.

---

[1] The order of the people still requires the sanction of the Senate for its ratification; but that sanction now being given beforehand, the order of the people is no longer subject to the control of the Senate, and therefore not precarious as heretofore.

18. The justice and piety of Numa Pompilius was at that time celebrated. He dwelt at Cures, a city of the Sabines, and was as eminently learned in all laws, human and divine, as any man could be in that age. They falsely represent that Pythagoras of Samos was his instructor in philosophy, because there appears no other person to refer to. Now, it is certain that this philosopher, in the reign of Servius Tullius, more than a hundred years after this, held assemblies of young men, who eagerly imbibed his doctrine, in the most distant part of Italy, about Metapontus, Heraclea and Croton. But from these places,[1] even had he flourished at the same time, what fame of his (extending) to the Sabines could have aroused any one to a desire of learning, or by what intercourse of language (could such a thing have been effected)? Besides, how could a single man have safely passed through so many nations differing in language and customs? I presume, therefore, that his mind was naturally furnished with virtuous dispositions, and that he was not so much versed in foreign sciences as in the severe and rigid discipline of the ancient Sabines, than which class none was in former times more strict. The Roman fathers, upon hearing the name of Numa, although they perceived that the scale of power would incline to the Sabines if a king were chosen from them, yet none of them ventured to prefer himself, or any other of his party, or any of the citizens or fathers, to that person, but unanimously resolved that the kingdom should be conferred on Numa Pompilius. Be-

---

[1] *Ex quibus locis, quæ fama in Sabinos, aut quo linguæ commercio—quenquam excivisset.* " From which (remote) places, what high character of him (could have reached) to the Sabines, or by what intercourse of language could such high character of him have aroused any one to become a pupil? " Other editions read *quâ famâ;* thus, from which places, by what high character for talent, or by what intercourse of language could he, Pythagoras, have aroused any one, etc. ?

ing sent for, just as Romulus before the building of the city
obtained the throne by an augury, he commanded the gods
to be consulted concerning himself also.   Upon this, being
conducted into the citadel by an augur (to which profession
that office was made a public one and perpetual by way of
honor), he sat down on a stone facing the south ; the augur
took his seat on his left hand with his head covered, holding in his right a crooked wand free from knots, which
they called *lituus;* then taking a view towards the city and
country, after offering a prayer to the gods, he marked out
the regions from east to west, the parts towards the south he
called the right, those towards the north, the left ; and in
front of him he set out in his mind a sign as far as ever his
eye could reach.   Then having shifted the lituus into his
left hand, placing his right hand on the head of Numa, he
prayed in this manner : "O father Jupiter, if it is thy will
that this Numa Pompilius, whose head I hold, should be
king of Rome, I beseech thee to give sure and evident signs
of it within those bounds which I have marked."   Then he
stated in set terms the omens which he wished to be sent ;
and on their being sent, Numa was declared king and came
down from the stand.

19. Having thus obtained the kingdom, he sets about establishing anew, on the principles of laws and morals, the
city recently established by violence and arms.   When he
saw that their minds, as having been rendered ferocious by
military life, could not be reconciled to those principles
during the continuance of wars, considering that a fierce
people should be mollified by the disuse of arms, he erected
at the foot of Argiletum a temple of Janus as an index of
peace and war ; that, when open, it might show the state
was engaged in war, and, when shut, that all the neighboring nations were at peace with it.   Twice only since the

reign of Numa hath this temple been shut; once when **T. Manlius** was consul, at the end of the first Punic war, and a second time, which the gods granted our age to see, by the emperor Augustus Cæsar, after the battle of Actium, peace being established by sea and land. This being shut, after he had secured the friendship of the neighboring states around by alliance and treaties, all anxiety regarding dangers from abroad being removed, lest their minds, which the fear of enemies and military discipline had kept in check, should become licentious by tranquillity, he considered that, first of all, an awe of the gods should be instilled into them, a principle of the greatest efficacy with a multitude ignorant and uncivilized as in those times. But as it could not sink deeply into their minds without some fiction of a miracle, he pretends that he holds nightly interviews with the goddess Egeria; that by her direction he instituted the sacred rites which would be most acceptable to the gods, and appointed proper priests for each of the deities. And, first of all, he divides the year into twelve months, according to the course of the moon; and because the moon does not make up thirty days in each month, and some days are wanting to the complete year as constituted by the solstitial revolution, he so portioned it out by inserting intercalary months that every twenty-fourth year, the lengths of all the intermediate years being completed, the days should correspond to the same place of the sun (in the heavens) whence they had set out.[1] He likewise made a distinction

[1] Romulus had made his year to consist of ten months, the first month being March, and the number of days in the year being only 304, which corresponded neither with the course of the sun nor moon. Numa, who added the two months of January and February, divided the year into twelve months, according to the course of the moon. This was the lunar Greek year, and consisted of 354 days. Numa, however, adopted 355 days for his year, from his partiality to

of the days[1] into profane and sacred, because on some it was likely to be expedient that no business should be transacted with the people.

20. Next he turned his attention to the appointment of priests, though he performed many sacred rites himself, especially those which now belong to the flamen of Jupiter. But, as he imagined that in a warlike nation there would be more kings resembling Romulus than Numa, and that they would go to war in person, he appointed a residentiary priest as flamen to Jupiter, that the sacred functions of the royal office might not be neglected, and he distinguished him by a fine robe, and a royal curule chair. To him he added two other flamines, one for Mars, another for Quirinus. He also

odd numbers. The lunar year of 354 days fell short of the solar year by $11\frac{1}{4}$ days; this in 8 years amounted to $(11\frac{1}{4} \times 8)$ 90 days. These 90 days he divided into 2 months of 22 and 2 of 23 days $(2 \times 22 + 2 \times 23 = 90)$, and introduced them alternately every second year for two octennial periods; every third octennial period, however, Numa intercalated only 66 days instead of 90 days, i.e., he inserted 3 months of only 22 days each. The reason was, because he adopted 355 days as the length of his lunar year instead of 354, and this in 24 years (3 octennial periods) produced an error of 24 days; this error was exactly compensated by intercalating only 66 days (90—24) in the third octennial period. The intercalations were generally made in the month of February, after the 23d of the month. Their management was left to the pontiffs—ad metam eandem solis unde orsi essent—dies congruerent; "that the days might correspond to the same starting-point of the sun in the heavens whence they had set out." That is, taking, for instance, the Tropic of Cancer for the place or starting-point of the sun any one year, and observing that he was in that point of the heavens on precisely the 21st of June, the object was so to dispense the year that the day on which the sun was observed to arrive at that same meta or starting-point again should also be called the 21st of June; such was the congruity aimed at by these intercalations.

[1] Ille nefastus erit per quem tria verba silentur;
   Fastus erit, per quem lege licebit agi.—Ov. F. i. 47.

selected virgins for Vesta, a priesthood derived from Alba, and not foreign to the family of the founder. That they might be constant attendants in the temple, he appointed them salaries out of the public treasury; and by enjoining virginity and other religious observances, he made them sacred and venerable. He selected twelve Salii for Mars Gradivus, and gave them the distinction of an embroidered tunic, and over the tunic a brazen covering for the breast. He commanded them to carry the celestial shields called Ancilia,[1] and to go through the city singing songs, with leaping and solemn dancing. Then he chose out of the number of the fathers Numa Marcius, son of Marcus, as pontiff,[2] and consigned to him an entire system of religious rites written out and sealed, (showing) with what victims, upon what days, and in what temples the sacred rites were to be performed; and from what funds the money was to be taken for these expenses. He placed all religious institutions, public and private, under the cognizance of the pontiff, to the end that there might be some place where the people should come to consult, lest any confusion in the divine worship might be occasioned by neglecting the ceremonies of their own country, and introducing foreign ones. (He ordained) that the same pontiff should instruct the people not only in the celestial ceremonies, but also in (the manner of performing) funeral solemnities, and of appeasing the manes of the dead; and what prodigies sent by lightning or any other phenomenon were to be attended to and expiated. To elicit such knowledge from the divine mind, he dedicated an altar on the Aventine to Jupiter Elicius,[3]

---

[1] *Ancilia*, from ἀγκυλος.   [2] *Pontificem*, scil. Maximum.

[3] *Eliciunt cælo te, Jupiter : unde minores*

  Nunc quoque te celebrant, Eliciumque vocant.—Ov. F. iii. 327.

and consulted the god by auguries as to what (prodigies) should be expiated.

21. The whole multitude having been diverted from violence and arms to the considering and adjusting these matters, both their minds had been engaged in doing something, and the constant watchfulness of the gods now impressed upon them, as the deity of heaven seemed to interest itself in human concerns, had filled the breasts of all with such piety, that faith and religious obligations governed the state, no less than fear of the laws and of punishment. And while[1] the people were moulding themselves after the morals of the king, as their best example, the neighboring states also, who had formerly thought that it was a camp, not a city, situate in the midst of them to disturb the general peace, were brought (to feel) such respect for them, that they considered it impious that a state wholly occupied in the worship of the gods should be molested. There was a grove, the middle of which was irrigated by a spring of running water, issuing from a dark grotto. As Numa went often thither alone, under pretense of conferring with the goddess, he dedicated the place to the Muses, because their meetings with his wife Egeria were held there. He also instituted a yearly festival to Faith alone, and commanded the priests to be carried to her temple in an arched chariot drawn by two horses, and to perform the divine service with their hands wrapt up to the fingers, intimating that Faith ought to be protected, and that her seat ought to be sacred even in

---

[1] *Cum ipsi se——formarent, tum finitimi etiam*, etc. Some of the editors of Livy have remarked on this passage, that *cum*, when answering to *tum*, may be joined to a subjunctive, as here ; the fact, however, is that *cum* here does not answer to *tum* at all ; *cum* is here " whilst "—and so necessarily requires the verb to be in the subjunctive mood.

men's right hands. He instituted many other sacred rites,
and dedicated places for performing them, which the priests
called Argei. But the greatest of all his works was his
maintenance of peace during the whole period of his reign,
no less than of his royal prerogative. Thus two kings in
succession, by different methods, the one by war, the other
by peace, aggrandized the state. Romulus reigned thirty-
seven years, Numa forty-three; the state was both strong
and well versed in the arts of war and peace.

22. Upon the death of Numa, the administration returned
again to an interregnum. After that the people appointed
as king Tullus Hostilius, the grandson of that Hostilius who
had made the noble stand against the Sabines at the foot of
the citadel. The fathers confirmed the choice. He was not
only unlike the preceding king, but was even of a more warlike disposition than Romulus. Both his youth and strength,
and the renown of his grandfather, stimulated his ambition.
Thinking, therefore, that the state was becoming languid
through quiet, he everywhere sought for pretexts for stir-
ring up war. It happened that some Roman and Alban
peasants had mutually plundered each other's lands. C.
Cluilius at that time governed Alba. From both sides ambassadors were sent almost at the same time, to demand restitution. Tullus ordered his to attend to nothing before
their instructions. He knew well that the Alban would refuse, and that so war might be proclaimed on just grounds.
Their commission was executed more remissly by the Albans. For being courteously and kindly entertained by
Tullus, they politely avail themselves of the king's hospitality. Meanwhile the Romans had both been first in demanding restitution, and, upon the refusal of the Albans,
had proclaimed war after an interval of thirty days ; of this
they give Tullus notice. Upon this he granted the Alban

ambassadors an opportunity of stating what they came to demand. They, ignorant of all, waste some time in making apologies: "That it was with the utmost reluctance they should say anything which was not pleasing to Tullus; but they were compelled by their orders. That they had come to demand restitution; and if this be not made, they were commanded to declare war." To this Tullus made answer: "Go tell your king that the king of the Romans takes the gods to witness which of the two nations hath with contempt first dismissed the ambassadors demanding restitution, that on it they may visit all the calamities of this war." The Albans carry home these tidings.

23. War was prepared for on both sides with the utmost vigor, very like to a civil war, in a manner between parents and children, both being Trojan offspring; for from Troy came Lavinium, from Lavinium Alba, and the Romans were descended from the race of Alban kings. But the result of the war rendered the quarrel less distressing, for they never came to any action; and when the houses only of one of the cities had been demolished, the two states were incorporated into one. The Albans first made an irruption into the Roman territories with a large army. They pitch their camp not above five miles from the city, and surround it with a trench which, for several ages, was called the Cluilian trench, from the name of the general, till, in process of time, the name, together with the thing itself, were both forgotten. In that camp Cluilius, the Alban king, dies; the Albans create Mettus[1] Fuffetius dictator. In the mean time, Tullus, being in high spirits, especially on the death of the king, and giving out that the supreme power of the gods

---

[1] *Mettus.* Gronovius and Bekker read *Mettius;* Niebuhr also prefers *Mettius;* he conceives that the Latin *prænomina* and the Roman *nomina* terminated in *ius.*

having begun at the head, would take vengeance on the
whole Alban nation for this impious war, having passed the
enemy's camp in the night-time, marches with a hostile army
into the Alban territory. This circumstance drew out Mettus from his camp likewise ; he leads his forces as near as he
can to the enemy ; from thence he commands a herald, dispatched by him, to tell Tullus that a conference was expedient before they came to an engagement ; and that if he would
give him a meeting, he was certain he should adduce matters which concerned the interest of Rome not less than that
of Alba.   Tullus, not slighting the proposal, though the
advances made were of little avail, draws out his men in order of battle ; the Albans, on their part, come out also. As
both armies stood in battle array, the chiefs, with a few of
the principal officers, advance into the middle between
them. Then the Alban commences thus : "That injuries
and the non-restitution of property according to treaty,
when demanded, were the cause of this war, methinks I both
heard our King Cluilius (assert), and I doubt not, Tullus,
but that you state the same thing.[1] But if the truth is to be
told, rather than that which is plausible, the desire of dominion stimulates two kindred and neighboring states to
arms. Nor do I take upon myself to determine whether
rightly or wrongly : be that his consideration who commenced the war. The Albans have made me their leader
for carrying on the war. Of this, Tullus, I would wish to
warn you ; how powerful the Etruscan state is around us,
and round you particularly, you know better (than we), inasmuch as you are nearer them. They are very powerful
by land, extremely so by sea. Recollect that, when you

---

[1] *Injurias et non redditas,* etc.   The construction is *et ego videor au-
disse regem nostrum Cluilium (præ se ferre) injurias et non redditas res
.........nec dubito te ferre eadem præ te, Tulle.*

3

shall give the signal for battle, these two armies will presently be a spectacle to them; and they may fall on us wearied and exhausted, victor and vanquished, together. Therefore, in the name of Heaven, since, not content with certain liberty, we are incurring the dubious risk of sovereignty and slavery, let us adopt some method whereby, without much loss, without much blood of either nation, it may be decided which shall rule the other." The proposal is not displeasing to Tullus, though both from the natural bent of his mind, as also from the hope of victory, he was rather inclined to violence. After some consideration, a plan is adopted on both sides, for which Fortune herself afforded the materials.

24. It happened that there were in each of the two armies three brothers[1] born at one birth, unequal neither in age nor strength. That they were called Horatii and Curiatii is certain enough; nor is there any circumstance of antiquity more celebrated; yet, in a matter so well ascertained, a doubt remains concerning their names, to which nation the Horatii and to which the Curiatii belonged. Authors claim them for both sides, yet I find more who call the Horatii Romans. My inclination leads me to follow them. The kings confer with the three brothers that they should fight with their swords, each in defence of their respective country, (assuring them) that dominion would be on that side on which victory should be. No objection is made; time and place are agreed on. Before they engaged, a compact is entered into between the Romans and Albans on these conditions, that the state whose champions should come off victorious in that combat should rule the other state without further dispute. Different treaties are made on different

[1] *Three brothers born at one birth.* Dionys. iii. 14, describes them as cousin-germans. Vid. Wachsmuth, p. 147. Niebuhr, i. p. 342.

terms, but they are all concluded in the same general method. We have heard that it was then concluded as follows, nor is there a more ancient record of any treaty: A herald asked King Tullus thus, "Do you command me, O king, to conclude a treaty with the pater patratus of the Alban people?" After the king had given command, he · said, "I demand vervain of thee, O king." To which the king replied, "Take some that is pure." The herald brought a pure blade of grass from the citadel; again he asked the king thus: "Dost thou, O king, appoint me the royal delegate of the Roman people, the Quirites, *including* my vessels and attendants?" The king answered, "That which may be done without detriment to me and to the Roman people, the Quirites, I do." The herald was M. Valerius, who appointed Sp. Fusius pater patratus, touching his head and hair with the vervain. The pater patratus is appointed "ad jusjurandum patrandum," that is, to ratify the treaty; and he goes through it in a great many words, which, being expressed in a long set form, it is not worth while repeating. After setting forth the conditions, he says: "Hear, O Jupiter; hear, O pater patratus of the Alban people, and ye, Alban people, hear. As those (conditions), from first to last, have been recited openly from those tablets of wax without wicked fraud, and as they have been most correctly understood here this day, from those conditions the Roman people will not be the first to swerve. If they first swerve by public concert, by wicked fraud, on that day do thou, O Jupiter, so strike the Roman people, as I shall here this day strike this swine; and do thou strike them so much the more, as thou art more able and more powerful." When he said this, he struck the swine with a flint stone. The Albans likewise went through their own form and oath by their own dictator and priests.

25. The treaty being concluded, the twin-brothers, as had been agreed, take arms.   While their respective friends exhortingly reminded each party "that their country's gods, their country and parents, all their countrymen both at home and in the army, had their eyes then fixed on their arms, on their hands; naturally brave, and animated by the exhortations of their friends, they advance into the midst between the two lines.   The two armies sat down before their respective camps, free rather from present danger than from anxiety; for the sovereign power was at stake, depending on the valor and fortune of so few."   Accordingly, therefore, eager and anxious, they have their attention intensely riveted on a spectacle far from pleasing.   The signal is given; and the three youths on each side, as if in battle array, rush to the charge with determined fury, bearing in their breasts the spirits of mighty armies: nor do the one or the other regard their personal danger; the public dominion or slavery is present to their mind, and the fortune[1] of their country, which was ever after destined .to be such as they should now establish it.   As soon as their arms clashed on the first encounter, and their burnished swords glittered, great horror strikes the spectators; and, hope inclining to neither side, their voice and breath were suspended.   Then having engaged hand to hand, when not only the movements of their bodies, and the rapid brandishings of their arms and weapons, but wounds also and blood were seen, two of the Romans fell lifeless, one upon the other, the three Albans being wounded.   And when the Alban army raised a shout of joy at their fall, hope entirely, anx-

---

[1] The order is: *fortuna patriæ deinde futura ea quam ipsi f. (animo obvers.)*; the fortune of their country, the high or humble character of which for the future depended on their exertions on that occasion.

iety, however, not yet, deserted the Roman legions, alarmed
for the lot of the one whom the three Curiatii surrounded.
He happened to be unhurt, so that though, alone, he was by
no means a match for them all together, yet he was confi-
dent against each singly. In order, therefore, to separate
their attack, he takes to flight, presuming that they would
pursue him with such swiftness as the wounded state of his
body would suffer each. He had now fled a considerable
distance from the place where they had fought, when, looking behind, he perceives them pursuing him at great inter-
vals from each other, and that one of them was not far from
him. On him he turned round with great fury. And while
the Alban army shouts out to the Curiatii to succor their
brother, Horatius, victorious in having slain his antagonist,
was now proceeding to a second attack. Then the Romans
encourage their champion with a shout such as is usually
(given) by persons cheering in consequence of unexpected
success ; he also hastens to put an end to the combat. Wherefore before the other, who was not far off, could come up,
he dispatches the second Curiatius also. And now, the
combat being brought to an equality of numbers, one on
each side remained, but they were equal neither in hope nor
in strength. The one, his body untouched by a weapon,
and a double victory made courageous for a third contest :
the other, dragging along his body exhausted from the
wound, exhausted from running, and dispirited by the
slaughter of his brethren before his eyes, presents himself
to his victorious antagonist. Nor was that a fight. The
Roman, exulting, says : "Two I have offered to the shades
of my brothers : the third I will offer to the cause of this
war, that the Roman may rule over the Alban." He
thrusts his sword down into his throat, while faintly sustaining the weight of his armor : he strips him as he lies

prostrate.   The Romans receive Horatius with triumph and congratulation ; with so much the greater joy, as success had followed so close on fear.   They then turn to the burial of their friends with dispositions by no means alike ; for the one side was elated with (the acquisition of) empire, the other subjected to foreign jurisdiction : their sepulchres are still extant in the place where each fell ; the two Roman ones in one place nearer to Alba, the three Alban ones towards Rome ; but distant in situation from each other, and just as they fought.[1]

26. Before they parted from thence, when Mettus, in conformity to the treaty which had been concluded, asked what orders he had to give, Tullus orders him to keep the youth in arms, that he designed to employ them if a war should break out with the Veientes.   After this both armies returned to their homes.   Horatius marched foremost, carrying before him the spoils of the three brothers ; his sister, a maiden who had been betrothed to one of the Curiatii, met him before the gate Capena ; and having recognized her lover's military robe, which she herself had wrought, on her brother's shoulders, she tore her hair, and with bitter wailings called by name on her deceased lover.   The sister's lamentations in the midst of his own victory, and of such great public rejoicings, raised the indignation of the excited youth.   Having therefore drawn his sword, he run the damsel through the body, at the same time chiding her in these words: "Go hence with thy unseasonable love to thy spouse, forgetful of thy dead brothers, and of him who survives, forgetful of thy native country.   So perish every Roman

---

[1] The two Roman champions, we have seen, fell in the one place, *super alium alius;* consequently, were buried together ; while the Curiatii fell in different places, as Horatius contrived to separate them to avoid their joint attack.

woman who shall mourn an enemy." This action seemed
shocking to the fathers and to the people; but his recent
services outweighed its guilt. Nevertheless he was carried
before the king for judgment. The king, that he himself
might not be the author of a decision so melancholy, and so
disagreeable to the people, or of the punishment consequent
on that decision, having summoned an assembly of the people, says, "I appoint, according to law, duumvirs to pass
sentence on Horatius for treason."[1] The law was of dreadful
import. "Let the duumvirs pass sentence for treason.[2] If
he appeal from the duumvirs, let him contend by appeal; if
they shall gain the cause,[3] cover his head; hang him by a
rope from a gallows; scourge him either within the Pomœrium or without the Pomœrium." When the duumvirs appointed by this law, who did not consider that, according to
the law, they could acquit even an innocent person,[4] had
found him guilty, one of them says, "P. Horatius, I judge
thee guilty of treason. Go, lictor, bind his hands." The
lictor had approached him, and was fixing the rope. Then
Horatius, by the advice of Tullus,[5] a favorable interpreter
of the law, says, "I appeal." Accordingly the matter was
contested by appeal to the people. On that trial persons
were much affected, especially by P. Horatius, the father,

[1] *Perduellio* (duellum, bellum), high treason against the state, or its
sovereign; but in those times any offense deserving capital punishment was included under that of treason, *Qui Horatio perduellionem
judicent*, to pass sentence on Horatius, as being manifestly guilty of
murder; not to try whether he was guilty or not.

[2] Duumviri, etc. Niebuhr considers these to be the very words of
the old formula.

[3] If the sentence (of the duumviri) be confirmed by the people.

[4] The letter of the law allowed of no justification or extenuation
of the fact. It left no alternative to the judge.

[5] He kindly pointed out the loop-hole in the law, which left an
opening for the culprit's acquittal.

declaring that he considered his daughter deservedly slain;
were it not so, that he would, by his authority as a father,
have inflicted punishment on his son.[1] He then entreated
that they would not render childless him whom but a little
while ago they had beheld with a fine progeny. During
these words the old man, having embraced the youth, point-
ing to the spoils of the Curiatii fixed up in that place which
is now called Pila Horatia—"Romans," said he, "can you
bear to see bound beneath the gallows amidst scourges and
tortures, him whom you just now beheld marching decorated
(with spoils) and exulting in victory; a sight so shocking as
the eyes even of the Albans could scarcely endure. Go, lictor, bind those hands which but a little while since, being
armed, established sovereignty for the Roman people. Go,
cover the head of the liberator of this city; hang him on
the gallows; scourge him, either within the Pomœrium, so
it be only amidst those javelins and spoils of the enemy; or
without the Pomœrium, only amidst the graves of the Curiatii. For whither can you bring this youth, where his own
glories must not redeem him from such ignominy of punishment?" The people could not withstand the tears of the
father or the resolution of the son, so undaunted in every
danger; and acquitted him more through admiration of his
bravery than for the justice of his cause. But that so notorious
a murder might be atoned for by some expiation, the father
was commanded to make satisfaction for the son at the public charge. He, having offered certain expiatory sacrifices,
which were ever after continued in the Horatian family, and
laid a beam across the street, made his son pass under it as
under a yoke, with his head covered. This remains even
to this day, being constantly repaired at the expense of the

[1] By the laws of Romulus, a father had the power of life and death
over his children.

public ; they call it Sororium Tigillum. A tomb of square stone was erected to Horatia in the place where she was stabbed and fell.

27. Nor did the peace with Alba continue long. The dissatisfaction of the populace, because the fortune of the state had been hazarded on three soldiers, perverted the weak mind of the dictator ; and because honorable measures had not turned out well, he began to conciliate their affections by perfidious means. Accordingly, as one formerly seeking peace in war, so now seeking war in peace, because he perceived that his own state possessed more courage than strength, he stirs up other nations to make war openly by proclamation ; for his own people he reserves treachery under the mask of alliance.[1] The Fidenates, a Roman colony, having gained over the Veientes as partisans in the confederacy, are instigated to declare war and take up arms under a compact of desertion on the part of the Albans. When Fidenæ had openly revolted,[2] Tullus, after summoning Mettus and his army from Alba, marches against the enemy. When he crossed the Anio, he pitches his camp at the conflux of the rivers.[3] Between that place and Fidenæ the army of the Veientes had crossed the Tiber. These, in line of battle, occupied the right wing near the river ; the Fidenates are posted on the left, nearer the mountains. Tullus stations his own men opposite the Veientian foe ; the Albans he opposes to the legion of the Fidenates. The Alban had not more courage than fidelity. Neither daring, there-

[1] The part which he reserves for himself and the Albans is to play the traitors to Tullus in the hour of need, wearing meanwhile the mark of friendship to Rome.

[2] The fact is, that the subject population rose up against the Roman colonists, drove them out of the town, and asserted their independence. Nieb. i. 24, 5.

[3] The Tiber and the Anio.

3 *

fore, to keep his ground, nor to desert openly, he files off slowly to the mountains. After this, when he supposed he had gone far enough, he halts[1] his entire army ; and being still irresolute in mind, in order to waste time, he opens his ranks. His design was to turn his forces to that side to which fortune should give success.   At first the Romans who stood nearest were astonished when they perceived their flanks were uncovered by the departure of their allies ; then a horseman in full gallop announces to the king that the Albans were moving off.   Tullus, in this perilous juncture, vowed twelve Salii, and temples to Paleness and Panic. Rebuking the horseman in a loud voice, so that the enemy might hear him, he orders him to return to the fight, " that there was no occasion for alarm ; that by his order the Alban army was marching round to fall on the unprotected rear of the Fidenates." He likewise commands him to order the cavalry to raise their spears aloft ; this expedient intercepted from a great part of the Roman infantry the view of the Alban army retreating.   Those who saw it, believing what they had heard the king say, fought with the greater ardor.   The alarm is now transferred to the enemy ; they had both heard what had been pronounced so audibly, and a great part of the Fidenates, as having been joined as colonists to the Romans, understood Latin.   Therefore, that they might not be intercepted from the town by a sudden descent of the Albans from the hills, they take to flight. Tullus presses forward, and, having routed the wing of the Fidenates, returned with greater fury against the Veientes, disheartened by the panic of the others : nor did they sustain his charge ; but the river, opposed to them behind, prevented a precipitate flight.   Whither when their flight led,

---

[1] *Erigit*—" he makes it halt," from the French *faire alte*, or formerly *haut*, because soldiers then stand upright and hold their spears erect.

some, shamefully throwing down their arms, rushed blindly
into the river; others, while they linger on the banks,
doubting whether to fly or fight, were overpowered. Never
before had the Romans a more desperate battle.

28. Then the Alban army, that had been spectators of the
fight, was marched down into the plains. Mettus congratu-
lates Tullus on his defeat of the enemy; Tullus, on his part,
addresses Mettus with great civility. He orders the Albans
to unite their camp with the Romans, which he prayed might
prove beneficial to both; and prepares a sacrifice of purifi-
cation for the next day. As soon as it was light, all things
being in readiness, according to custom, he commands both
armies to be summoned to an assembly. The heralds, beginning at the outside,[1] summoned the Albans first. They,
struck too[2] with the novelty of the thing, in order to hear
the Roman king harangue, crowded next to him. The
Roman legions, under arms, by concert surrounded them; a
charge had been given to the centurions to execute their
orders without delay. Then Tullus begins as follows : " Romans, if ever before at any other time in any war there was
(an occasion) on which you should return thanks, first to
the immortal gods, next to your own valor, that occasion
was yesterday's battle. For the contest was not more with
enemies than with the treachery and perfidy of allies, a contest which is more serious and more dangerous. For that a
false opinion may not influence you, the Albans retired to the
mountains without my orders; nor was that my command,
but a stratagem and the pretense of a command; that so
your attention might not be drawn away from the fight, you
being kept in ignorance that you were deserted, and that

[1] *Præcones ab extremo.* At the farther part of the Roman camp,
where it joined that of the Albans.
[2] As well as by the orders issued by Tullus.

terror and dismay might be struck into the enemy, conceiving themselves to be surrounded on the rear. Nor does that guilt, which I now state, extend to all the Albans. They followed their leader, as you too would have done if I had wished my army to make a move to any other point from thence. Mettus there is the leader of that march—the same Mettus is the contriver of this war; Mettus is the violator of the treaty between Rome and Alba. Let another hereafter attempt the like conduct, unless I now make of him a signal example to mankind." The centurions in arms stand round Mettus, and the king proceeds with the rest as he had commenced : "It is my intention, and may it prove fortunate, auspicious and happy to the Roman people, to myself and to you, O Albans, to transplant all the inhabitants of Alba to Rome ; to grant your people the rights of citizenship, and to admit your nobles into the rank of Senators ; to make one city, one republic ; that as the Alban state was formerly divided from one people into two, so it may now return into one." On hearing this, the Alban youth, unarmed, surrounded by armed men, however divided in their sentiments, yet restrained by the common apprehension, continue silent. Then Tullus proceeded : "If, Mettus Fuffetius, you were capable of learning fidelity, and how to observe treaties, that lesson would have been taught you by me while still alive. Now, since your disposition is incurable, do you at least, by your punishment, teach mankind to consider those things sacred which have been violated by you. As, therefore, a little while since you kept your mind divided between the interest of Fidenæ and of Rome, so shall you now surrender your body to be torn asunder in different directions." Upon this, two chariots, drawn by four horses, being brought, he ties Mettus, extended at full length, to their carriages ; then the horses

were driven on in different directions, carrying off the man-
gled body on each carriage, where the limbs had been fas-
tened by the cords. All turned away their eyes from so
shocking a spectacle. That was the first and last instance
of a punishment among the Romans regardless of the laws
of humanity. In other cases we may boast that no nation
whatever adopted milder forms of punishment.

29. During these occurrences the cavalry had been dispatched onward to Alba to remove the multitude to Rome.
The legions were next led thither to demolish the city.
When they entered the gates there was not, indeed, that
tumult nor panic, such as usually takes place with captured
cities when, the gates being burst open, or the walls levelled
by the ram, or the citadel taken by assault, the shouts of
the enemy and rush of armed men through the city throws
every thing into confusion by fire and sword; but gloomy
silence and speechless sorrow so absorbed the minds of all
that, through fear, forgetting what they should leave behind, what they should take with them, all concert failing
them, and frequently making inquiries of each other, they
now stood at their thresholds, now wandering about, they
strayed through their houses, doomed to see them for the
last time. But as soon as the shouts of the horsemen commanding them to depart now urged them on, the crashing
of the dwellings which were being demolished was now
heard in the remotest parts of the city, and the dust, rising
in distant places, had filled every quarter as with a cloud
spread over them ; hastily snatching up whatever each of
them could, while they went forth leaving behind them
their guardian deity and household gods and the homes in
which each had been born and brought up, a continued
train of emigrants soon filled the ways, and the sight of
others, through mutual commiseration, renewed their tears;

and piteous cries, too, were heard, of the women more especially, when they passed by their revered temples, now
beset with armed men, and left their gods, as it were, in
captivity. After the Albans had evacuated the town the
Roman soldiery level all the public and private edifices indiscriminately to the ground, and one short hour consigned to
demolition and ruin the work of four hundred years, during
which Alba had stood. The temples of the gods, however,
for such had been the orders given by the king, were spared.

30. In the mean time Rome increases by the demolition of
Alba. The number of citizens is doubled. The Cœlian
mount is added to the city, and, in order that it might be
inhabited more populously, Tullus selects that situation for
his palace, and there took up his abode. The leading persons among the Albans he enrolls among the patricians, that
that branch of the state also might increase—the Julii, Ser-
vilii, Quinctii, Geganii, Curiatii, Clœlii ; and as a consecrated
place of meeting for the order augmented by him he built a
Senate-house, which was called Hostilia even down to the
age of our fathers. And that every rank might acquire
some additional strength from the new people, he formed
ten troops of horsemen from among the Albans ; he likewise
recruited the old, and raised new legions from the same
source. Confiding in this increase of strength, Tullus declares war against the Sabines, a nation at that time the
most powerful, next to the Etrurians, in men and in arms.
Injuries had been done on both sides, and restitution demanded in vain. Tullus complained that some Roman merchants had been seized in an open market near the temple
of Feronia ; the Sabines, that some of their people had
taken refuge in the asylum and were detained at Rome.
These were assigned as the causes of the war. The Sabines,
holding in recollection both that a portion of their strength

had been fixed at Rome by Tatius, and that the Roman
power had also been lately increased by the accession of the
Alban people, began, on their part, to look around for foreign aid.   Etruria was in their neighborhood ; of the Etrurians the Veientes were the nearest.   From thence they drew
some volunteers, their minds being stirred up to a revolt,
chiefly in consequence of the rankling animosities from
(former) wars.   And pay also had its weight with some
stragglers belonging to the indigent population.   They were
assisted by no aid from the government, and the faith of the
truce stipulated with Romulus was strictly observed by the
Veientes (for with respect to the others it is less surprising).
While they were preparing for war with the utmost vigor,
and the matter seemed to turn on this, which should first
commence hostilities, Tullus first passes into the Sabine territory.   A desperate battle ensued at the wood called Mali-
tiosa,[1] in which the Roman army was far superior, both by
the strength of their foot and also by the recent augmenta-
tion of their cavalry.   The Sabine ranks were thrown into
disorder by a sudden charge of the cavalry ; nor could either
the fight be afterwards restored or a retreat accomplished
without great slaughter.

31. After the defeat of the Sabines, when the government
of Tullus and the whole Roman state was in high renown
and in a very flourishing condition, word was brought to
the king and Senators that it rained stones on the Alban
Mount.   As this could scarcely be credited, on persons being sent to inquire into the prodigy, a thick shower of stones
fell from heaven in their sight, just as when hail collected
into balls is pelted down to the earth by the winds.   Besides, they imagined that they heard a loud voice from the

---

[1] *Malitiosam.* Τὴν ὕλην καλουμένην Κακούργου. Dio. iii.

grove on the summit of the hill, requiring the Albans to perform their religious service according to the rites of their native country, which they had consigned to oblivion, as if their gods had been abandoned together with their country ; and they had either adopted the religion of Rome, or, as may happen, enraged at their evil destiny, had renounced altogether the worship of the gods. A festival of nine days was instituted publicly by the Romans also, on account of the same prodigy, either in obedience to the heavenly voice sent from the Alban mount (for that too is stated) or by the advice of the aruspices. Certain it is, it continued a solemn observance, that whenever the same prodigy was announced a festival for nine days was observed. Not long after, they were afflicted with a pestilence ; and though from this there arose an aversion to military service, yet no respite from arms was granted by this warlike king, who considered that the bodies of the young men were even more healthy abroad than at home, until he himself also was seized with a lingering disease. Then, together with his body, those fierce spirits became so broken, that he, who formerly considered nothing less worthy of a king than to devote his mind to religion, suddenly became a slave to every form of superstition, important and trifling, and filled the people's minds also with religious scruples. The generality of persons, now wishing to recur to that state of things which had existed under King Numa, thought that the only relief left for their sickly bodies was, if peace and pardon could be obtained from the gods. They say that the king himself, turning over the commentaries of Numa, after he had found therein that certain sacrifices of a secret and solemn nature had been performed to Jupiter Elicius, shut himself up and set about the performance of this solemnity ; but that that rite was not duly undertaken or conducted, and that not only no

appearance of heavenly notification was presented to him,
but that he was struck with lightning and burnt to ashes,
together with his house, through the anger of Jupiter, exasperated at the impropriety of the ceremony. Tullus
reigned two-and-thirty years with great military renown.

32. On the death of Tullus the government devolved once
more upon the Senate, and they nominated an interrex ; and
on his holding the comitia, the people elected Ancus Marcius
king. The fathers confirmed the election. Ancus Marcius
was the grandson of King Numa Pompilius by his daughter.
As soon as he ascended the throne, reflecting on the renown
of his grandfather, and that the late reign, glorious in every
other respect, in one particular had not been sufficiently
prosperous, the rites of religion having been either utterly
neglected or improperly performed ; deeming it of the highest importance to perform the public ceremonies of religion
as they had been instituted by Numa, he orders the pontiff,
after he had transcribed them all from the king's commentaries on white tables, to expose them to public view. Hence
both his own subjects, desirous of peace, and the neighboring nations, entertained a hope that the king would conform
to the conduct and institutions of his grandfather. Accordingly, the Latins, with whom a treaty had been concluded
in the reign of Tullus, assumed new courage ; and after they
had made an incursion upon the Roman lands, return a
contemptuous answer to the Romans on their demanding
restitution, supposing that the Roman king would spend his
reign in indolence among chapels and altars. The genius
of Ancus was of a middle kind, partaking both of that of
Numa and of Romulus ; and, besides that, he thought that
peace was more necessary in his grandfather's reign, considering the people were but recent as well as uncivilized,
he also (considered) that he could not, without injury, pre-

serve the tranquillity which had fallen to his lot; that his patience was tried, and, being tried, was now despised; and that the times were more suited to a King Tullus than to a Numa. In order, however, that as Numa had instituted religious rites in peace, ceremonies relating to war might be transmitted by him, and that wars might not only be waged, but proclaimed also according to some rite, he borrowed from an ancient nation, the Æquicolæ, the form which the heralds still preserve, according to which restitution is demanded. The ambassador, when he comes to the frontiers of the people from whom satisfaction is demanded, having his head covered with a fillet (the fillet is of wool), says: "Hear, O Jupiter, hear, ye confines (naming the nation they belong to), let Justice hear. I am a public messenger of the Roman people; I come justly and religiously deputed, and let my words gain credit." He then makes his demands; afterwards he makes a solemn appeal to Jupiter: "If I unjustly or impiously demand those persons and those goods to be given up to me, the messenger of the Roman people, then never permit me to enjoy my native country." These words he repeats when he passes over the frontiers; the same to the first man he meets; the same on entering the gate; the same on entering the Forum, some few words in the form of the declaration and oath being changed. If the persons whom he demands are not delivered up on the expiration of thirty-three days, for so many are enjoined by the rule, he declares war, thus: "Hear, Jupiter, and thou, Juno, Romulus, and all ye celestial, terrestrial, and infernal gods, give ear! I call you to witness that this nation (naming it) is unjust, and does not act with equity; but we will consult the fathers in our own country concerning these matters, and by what means we may obtain our right." After that the messenger returns to Rome to consult: the

king immediately used to consult the fathers almost in the
following words : "Concerning such matters, differences,
and quarrels, as the pater patratus of the Roman people,
the Quirites, has conferred with the pater patratus of the
ancient Latins, and with the ancient Latin people, which
matters ought to be given up, performed, discharged, which
matters they have neither given up, performed, nor discharged, declare," says he to him, whose opinion he first
asked, "What think you ?"   Then he said : "I think that
they should be demanded by a just and regularly declared
war, therefore I consent, and vote for it."   Then the others
were asked in order, and when the majority of those present
agreed in the same opinion, the war was resolved on.   It
was customary for the fecialis to carry in his hand a javelin
pointed with steel, or burnt at the end and dipped in blood,
to the confines of the enemy's country, and in presence of
at least three grown-up persons, to say : "Forasmuch as the
states of the ancient Latins, and the ancient Latin people,
have offended against the Roman people, the Quirites ; forasmuch as the Roman people, the Quirites, have ordered
that there should be war with the ancient Latins, and the
Senate of the Roman people, the Quirites, have given their
opinion, consented, and voted that war should be made with
the ancient Latins, on this account I and the Roman people
declare and make war on the states of the ancient Latins,
and on the ancient Latin people."   After he had said that,
he threw the spear within their confines.   After this manner
restitution was demanded from the Latins at that time, and
war proclaimed ; and that usage posterity have adopted.

33. Ancus, having committed the care of sacred things to
the flamines and other priests, set out with a new army,
which he had levied, and took Politorium, a city of the
Latins, by storm ; and following the example of former

kings, who had increased the Roman state by taking enemies into the number of the citizens, he transplanted all the
people to Rome. And since the Sabines occupied the Capitol and citadel, and the Albans the Cœlian mount around
the Palatium, the residence of the old Romans, the Aventine was assigned to the new people; not long after, on
Telleni and Ficana being taken, new citizens were added in
the same quarter. After this, Politorium was taken a second
time by force of arms, because the ancient Latins had taken
possession of it when vacated. This was the cause of the
Romans demolishing that city, that it might not ever after
serve as a receptacle to the enemy. At last, the whole war
with the Latins being concentrated in Medullia, they fought
there with various fortune, sometimes the one and sometimes
the other gaining the victory; for the town was both well
fortified by works and strengthened by a strong garrison,
and the Latins, having pitched their camp in the open
fields, had several times fought the Romans in close engagement. At last Ancus, making an effort with all his forces,
obtained a complete victory over them in a pitched battle,
and having got a considerable booty, returned thence to
Rome; many thousands of the Latins being then also admitted into the city, to whom, in order that the Aventine
might be joined to the Palatium, a settlement was assigned
near the temple of Murcia. The Janiculum was likewise
added, not for want of room, but lest at any time it should
become a lodgment for the enemy. It was determined to
join it to the city, not only by a wall, but likewise, for the
sake of the convenience of passage, by a wooden bridge,
then for the first time built across the Tiber. The Fossa
Quiritium, no inconsiderable defense against the easy access
to the city from the low grounds, is the work of King Ancus.
The state being augmented by such great accessions, seeing

that, amidst such a multitude of persons, the distinction of
right and wrong being as yet confounded, clandestine crimes
were committed, a prison is built in the heart of the city,
overlooking the Forum, to intimidate the growing licentiousness.   And not only was the city increased under this
king, but the territory also, and the boundaries.   The Mæ-
sian forest was taken from the Veientes, the Roman dominion was extended as far as the sea, and the city of Ostia built
at the mouth of the Tiber; salt-pits were formed around it,
and, in consequence of the distinguished success achieved
in war, the temple of Jupiter Feretrius was enlarged.

34. In the reign of Ancus, Lucumo, a rich and enterpris-
ing man, came to settle at Rome, prompted chiefly by the
desire and hope of obtaining great preferment there, which
he had no means of attaining at Tarquinii (for there also he
was descended from an alien stock).   He was the son of
Demaratus, a Corinthian, who, flying his country for sedition, had happened to settle at Tarquinii, and having married a wife there, had two sons by her.   Their names were
Lucumo[1] and Aruns.   Lucumo survived his father, and became heir to all his property.   Aruns died before his father,
leaving a wife pregnant.   The father did not long survive
the son; and as he, not knowing that his daughter-in-law
was pregnant, died without taking any notice of his grand-
child in his will, to the boy that was born after the death of
his grandfather, without having any share in his fortune,
the name of Egerius was given on account of his poverty.
And when his wealth already inspired Lucumo, on the other
hand, the heir of all his father's wealth, with elevated notions, Tanaquil, whom he married, further increased such

---

[1] The Lucumones were a class of persons among the Etrurians of a
warlike sacerdotal character, patricians, not kings. Vid. Niebuhr, i.
p. 372.

feeling, she being descended from a very high family, and
one who would not readily brook the condition into which
she had married to be inferior to that in which she had
been born. As the Etrurians despised Lucumo, because
sprung from a foreign exile, she could not bear the affront,
and regardless of the innate love of her native country, provided she might see her husband advanced to honors, she
formed the determination to leave Tarquinii.   Rome seemed
particularly suited for her purpose.   In this state, lately
founded, where all nobility is recent and the result of merit,
there would be room for her husband, a man of courage and
activity. Tatius, a Sabine, had been king of Rome: Numa
had been sent for from Cures to reign there: Ancus was
sprung from a Sabine mother, and rested his nobility on the
single statue of Numa. She easily persuades him, as being
ambitious of honors, and one to whom Tarquinii was his
country only on the mother's side.   Accordingly, removing
their effects, they set out together for Rome. They happened to have reached the Janiculum; there, as he sat in
the chariot with his wife, an eagle, suspended on her wings,
gently stooping, takes off his cap, and, flying round the
chariot with loud screams, as if she had been sent from
heaven for the very purpose, orderly replaced it on his
head, and then flew aloft.   Tanaquil is said to have received
this omen with great joy, being a woman well skilled, as the
Etrurians generally are, in celestial prodigies, and, embracing her husband, bids him hope for high and elevated fortune: that such bird had come from such a quarter of the
heavens, and the messenger of such a god; that it had exhibited the omen around the highest part of man; that it
had lifted the ornament placed on the head of man, to restore it to the same, by direction of the gods. Carrying
with them these hopes and thoughts, they entered the city,

and, having purchased a house there, they gave out the name of Lucius Tarquinius Priscus. His being a stranger and very rich, caused him to be taken notice of by the Romans. He also promoted his own good-fortune by his affable address, by the courteousness of his invitations, and by conciliating those whom he could by acts of kindness; until a report of him reached even to the palace; and by paying court to the king with politeness and address, he in a short time so improved the acquaintance to the footing of intimate friendship, that he was present at all public and private deliberations, foreign and domestic; and being now tried in every trust, he was at length, by the king's will, appointed guardian to his children.

35. Ancus reigned twenty-four years, equal to any of the former kings both in the arts and renown of war and peace. His sons were now nigh the age of puberty; for this reason Tarquin was more urgent that the assembly for the election of a king should be held as soon as possible. The assembly being proclaimed, he sent away the boys to hunt towards the time of their meeting. He is said to have been the first who earnestly sued for the crown, and to have made a set speech for the purpose of gaining the affections of the people: *he said* "that he did not aim at any thing unprecedented; for that he was not the first foreigner (a thing at which any one might feel indignation or surprise), but the third, who aspired to the sovereignty of Rome. That Tatius not only, from being an alien, but even an enemy, was made king; that Numa, unacquainted with the city, and without soliciting it, had been voluntarily invited by them to the throne; that he, as soon as he was his own master, had come to Rome with his wife and whole fortune, and had there spent a greater part of that age in which men are employed in civil offices than he had in his native country; that he had, both ·

in peace and war, thoroughly learned the Roman laws and
religious customs under a master not to be objected to, King
Ancus himself; that he had vied with all in duty and loyalty
to his prince, and even with the king himself in his bounty
to others." While he was recounting these undoubted facts,
the people by a great majority elected him king. The same
ambition which had prompted Tarquin, in other respects an
excellent man, to aspire to the crown, followed him while
on the throne. And being no less mindful of strengthening
his own power than of increasing that of the commonwealth,
he elected a hundred into the fathers, who from that time
were called Minorum Gentium, *i.e.*, of the younger families: a party hearty in the king's cause, by whose favor they
had got into the Senate. The first war he waged was with
the Latins, from whom he took the town of Apiolæ by
storm, and, having brought back thence more booty than
the character of the war would lead one to expect, he celebrated games with more cost and magnificence than former
kings. The place for the circus, which is now called Maximus, was then first marked out, and spaces were parted off
for the Senators and knights, where they might each erect
seats for themselves: they were called fori (benches). They
viewed the games from scaffolding which supported seats
twelve feet high from the ground. The show took place;
horses and boxers were sent for, chiefly from Etruria.
These solemn games afterwards continued annual, being
variously called the Roman and Great (games). By the
same king, also, spaces round the Forum were portioned off
for private individuals to build on; porticoes and shops
were erected.

  36. He was also preparing to surround the city with a
stone wall, when a Sabine war obstructed his designs. The
matter was so sudden, that the enemy had passed the Anio

before the Roman army could meet and stop them; great
alarm, therefore, was produced at Rome.   And at first they
fought with dubious success, but with great slaughter on
both sides.   After this, the enemy's forces being led back
into their camp, and the Romans getting time to make new
levies for the war, Tarquin, thinking that the weakness of
his army lay in the want of horse, determined to add other
centuries to the Ramnenses, the Titienses, and Luceres
which Romulus had appointed, and to leave them distinguished by his own name.   Because Romulus had done this
by augury, Attus Navius, at that time a celebrated sooth-
sayer, insisted that no alteration or new appointment of that
kind could be made unless the birds approved of it.   The
king, enraged at this, and, as it is related, ridiculing the
art, said: "Come, thou diviner, tell me, whether what I
am thinking on can be done or not?"   When he had tried
the matter by divination, he affirmed it certainly could.
"But I was thinking," says he, "whether you could cut
asunder this whetstone with a razor.   Take it, and perform
what thy birds portend may be done."   Upon this, as they
say, he immediately cut the whetstone in two.   A statue of
Attus, with his head veiled, was erected in the comitium,
upon the very steps on the left of the Senate-house, on the
spot where the transaction occurred.   They say that the
whetstone also was deposited in the same place, that it
might remain a monument of that miracle to posterity.
There certainly accrued so much honor to augury and the
college of augurs, that nothing was undertaken, either in
peace or war, without taking the auspices.   Assemblies of
the people, the summoning of armies, and affairs of the
greatest importance were put off, when the birds would not
allow of them.   Nor did Tarquin then make any other
alteration in the centuries of horse, except doubling the

4

number of men in each of these corps, so that the three centuries consisted of one thousand eight hundred knights. Those that were added were called "the younger," but by the same names with the former; which, now that they have been doubled, they call six centuries.

37. This part of his forces being augmented, a second battle is fought with the Sabines. But, besides that the Roman army was thus reinforced, a stratagem also is secretly resorted to, persons having been sent to throw into the river a great quantity of timber that lay on the banks of the Anio, it being first set on fire; and the wood being further kindled by favor of the wind, and the greater[1] part of it (being placed) on rafts, when it stuck firmly impacted against the piers, sets the bridge on fire. This accident struck terror into the Sabines during the battle, and, after they were routed, impeded their flight; so that many who had escaped the enemy perished in the river. Their arms floating down the Tiber, and being recognized at the city, made known the victory, almost before any account of it could be carried there. In that action the glory of the cavalry was prominent : they say that, being posted in the two wings, when the centre of their own infantry was being beaten, they charged so briskly in flank, that they not only checked the Sabine legions who pressed hard on those who retired,

---

[1] In my version of this passage I have followed the reading *et pleraque in ratibus, impacta sublicis quum hærerent*, p. i. The burning logs were not sent down the river one by one, but were placed on rafts, so that, being incapable of passing on between the piers of the bridge, they firmly stuck there, and burnt the bridge. This mode of interpretation is confirmed by Dion. iii., 5, 6. The bridge here meant is the one built by the Sabines at the confluence of the Anio and the Tiber.——Another reading is, *pleraque in ratibus impacta subliciis quam hærerent*, "most of them being driven against the boats, resting on piles, stuck there," etc.

but quickly put them to flight. The Sabines made for the mountains with great precipitation, yet few reached them ; for, as we said before, the greatest part were driven by the cavalry into the river. Tarquin, thinking it advisable to pursue the enemy closely, while in this consternation, after sending the booty and the prisoners to Rome, piling up and burning the spoils which he had vowed to Vulcan, proceeds to lead his army onward into the Sabine territory. And though matters had turned out adversely, nor could they hope for better success ; yet, because the occasion did not allow time for deliberation, the Sabines came out to meet him with a hastily raised army ; and being again defeated there, and matters having now become desperate, they sued for peace.

38. Collatia and all the land about it was taken from the Sabines, and Egerius, son to the king's brother, was left there with a garrison. I understand that the people of Collatia were thus surrendered, and that the form of the surrender was as follows : the king asked them, "Are ye ambassadors and deputies sent by the people of Collatia to surrender yourselves and the people of Collatia?" "We are." "Are the people of Collatia their own masters?" "They are." "Do ye surrender yourselves and the people of Collatia, their city, lands, water, boundaries, temples, utensils, and everything sacred or profane belonging to them, into my power and that of the Roman people?" "We do." "Then I receive them." The Sabine war being ended, Tarquin returned in triumph to Rome. After that he made war upon the ancient Latins, where they came on no occasion to a general engagement ; yet, by carrying about his arms to the several towns, he subdued the whole Latin nation. Corniculum, old Ficulea, Cameria, Crustumerium, Ameriola, Medullia, and Nomentum, towns which either be-

longed to the ancient Latins, or which had revolted to them, were taken. Upon this a peace was concluded. The works of peace were then set about with greater spirit even than the efforts with which he had conducted his wars; so that the people enjoyed no more ease and quiet at home than they had done abroad; for he both set about surrounding the city with a stone wall on the side where he had not fortified it, the beginning of which work had been interrupted by the Sabine war, and the lower parts of the city round the Forum, and the other valleys lying between the hills, because they did not easily carry off the water from the flat grounds, he drains by means of sewers drawn sloping downward into the Tiber. Moreover, he levels an area for founding a temple to Jupiter in the Capitol, which he had vowed to him in the Sabine war; his mind even then presaging the future grandeur of the place. ·

39. At that time a prodigy occurred in the palace wonderful both in its appearance and in its result. They relate that the head of a boy, called Servius Tullius, as he lay fast asleep, blazed with fire in the sight of many persons; that, by the very great noise made at so miraculous a phenomenon, the royal family were awakened; and when one of the servants was bringing water to extinguish the flame, that he was kept back by the queen, and, after the confusion was over, that she forbade the boy to be disturbed till he should awake of his own accord. As soon as he awoke the flame disappeared. Then Tanaquil, taking her husband into a private place, said: "Do you observe this boy whom we bring up in so mean a style? Be assured that hereafter he will be a light to us in our adversity, and a protector to our palace in distress. From henceforth let us, with all our care, train up this youth, who is capable of becoming a great ornament publicly and privately." From

this time the boy began to be treated as their own son, and
instructed in those arts by which men's minds are qualified
to maintain high rank. The matter was easily accomplished, because it was agreeable to the gods. The young
man turned out to be of a disposition truly royal. Nor,
when they looked out for a son-in-law for Tarquin, could
any of the Roman youth be compared to him in any accom-
plishment; therefore the king betrothed his own daughter
to him. This high honor conferred upon him, from whatever cause, prevents us from believing that he was the son
of a slave, and that he had himself been a slave when young.
I am rather of the opinion of those who say that, on the
taking of Corniculum, the wife of Servius Tullius, who had
been the leading man in that city, being pregnant when her·
husband was slain, being known among the other female
prisoners, and, in consequence of her high rank, exempted
from servitude by the Roman queen, was delivered of a
child at Rome, in the house of Tarquinius Priscus. Upon
this, that both the intimacy between the ladies was improved by so great a kindness, and that the boy, having
been brought up in the house from his infancy, was beloved
and respected; that his mother's lot, in having fallen into
the hands of the enemy, caused him to be considered the
son of a slave.

40. About the thirty-eighth year of Tarquin's reign, Servius Tullius was in the highest esteem, not only with the
king, but also with the Senate and people. At this time
the two sons of Ancus, though they had before that always
considered it the highest indignity that they had been deprived of their father's crown by the treachery of their
guardian, that a stranger should be king of Rome, who was
not only not of a civic, but not even of an Italian family, yet
now felt their indignation rise to a still higher pitch at the

notion that the crown would not only not revert to them
after Tarquin, but would descend even lower to a slave, so
that in the same state about the hundreth year[1] after Romulus,
descended from a deity, and a deity himself, occupied the
throne, as long as he lived, a slave, and one born of a slave,
should now possess it.   That it would be a disgrace both
common to the Roman name, and more especially to their
family, if, while there was male issue of King Ancus still
living, the sovereignty of Rome should be accessible not
only to strangers, but even to slaves.   They determine,
therefore, to prevent that disgrace by the sword.   But both
resentment for the injury done to them incensed them more
against Tarquin himself than against Servius, and the (consideration) that a king was likely to prove a more severe
avenger of the murder, if he should survive, than a private
person ; and moreover, in case of Servius being put to death,
whatever other person he might select as his son-in-law,[2] it
seemed likely that he would adopt as his successor on the
throne.[3]   For these reasons the plot is laid against the king

---

[1] *The hundreth year.* 138 years had elasped since the death of Romulus : they diminish the number of years designedly, to make the
matter appear still worse.

[2] *Son-in-law.* Why not one of his two sons, Lucius and Aruns?
Dio. iv. 1. If these were not his grandchildren rather, they must
have been infants at the time. Dio. iv. 4, 6.—At this time infants
could not succeed to the throne.—*Ruperti.*

[3] This sentence has given some trouble to the commentators.—Some
will have it that three distinct reasons are given for assassinating
Tarquinius rather than Servius Tullius, and that these are severally
marked and distinguished by *et—et—tum*, the second only having
quia.—Stroth will have it that only two reasons are assigned, one why
the king should be killed, and the other why Servius Tullius should
not be killed, arising from the danger and uselessness of the act—
the former has not a *quia*, because it was a fact (*et injuriæ dolor*, etc.).
while the latter has it in the first part (the danger, *et quia gravior*,
etc., *quia* being understood also before the other, the uselessness,

himself. Two of the most ferocious of the shepherds being
selected for the daring deed, with the rustic implements to
which each had been accustomed, by conducting themselves
in as violent a manner as possible in the porch of the
palace, under pretense of a quarrel, draw the attention of
all the king's attendants to themselves; then, when both
appealed to the king, and their clamor reached even the
interior of the palace, they are called in and proceed before
the king. At first both bawled aloud, and vied in interrupting each other by their clamor, until, being restrained by
the lictor, and commanded to speak in turns, they at length
cease railing. According to concert, one begins to state the
matter. When the king, attentive to him, had turned himself quite that way, the other, raising up his axe, struck it
into his head, and, leaving the weapon in the wound, they
both rush out of the house.

41. When those who were around had raised up the king
in a dying state, the lictors seize on the men who were en-
deavoring to escape. Upon this followed an uproar and
concourse of people, wondering what the matter was. Tanaquil, during the tumult, orders the palace to be shut, thrusts
out all who were present; at the same time, she sedulously
prepares every thing necessary for dressing the wound, as
if a hope still remained; at the same time, in case her hopes
should disappoint her, she projects other means of safety.
Sending immediately for Servius, after she had showed to
him her husband almost expiring, holding his right hand,

tum, Serviò occiso, etc.), because it contained the reasoning of the
youths. Doering says there were only two powerful reasons, revenge
and fear, and a ratio probabilis introduced by *tum;* which has the
force of insuper. According to Dr. Hunter, there are two formal as-
sertions; one, that resentment stimulated the sons of Ancus against
the king himself; the other, that the plot is laid for the king himself upon two considerations, of reason and policy.

she entreats him not to suffer the death of his father-in-law
to pass unavenged, nor his mother-in-law to be an object of
insult to their enemies. "Servius," she said, "if you are
a man, the kingdom is yours, not theirs, who, by the hands
of others, have perpetrated the worst of crimes. Exert
yourself, and follow the guidance of the gods, who portended that this head would be illustrious by having formerly shed a blaze around it. Now let that celestial flame
arouse you. Now awake in earnest. We, too, though
foreigners, have reigned. Consider who your are, not
whence you are sprung. If your own plans are not matured
by reason of the suddenness of this event, then follow
mine." When the uproar and violence of the multitude
could scarcely be withstood, Tanaquil addresses the populace from the upper part of the palace through the windows
facing the new street (for the royal family resided near the
Temple of Jupiter Stator). She bids them " be of good
courage ; that the king was stunned by the suddenness of
the blow ; that the weapon had not sunk deep into his
body ; that he was already come to himself again ; that the
wound had been examined, the blood having been wiped off ;
that all the symptoms were favorable ; that she hoped they
would see him very soon ; and that, in the mean time, he
commanded the people to obey the orders of Servius Tullius.
That he would administer justice, and would perform all
the functions of the king." Servius comes forth with the
trabea and lictors, and, seating himself on the king's throne,
decides some cases, with respect to others pretends that he
will consult the king. Therefore, the death being concealed for several days, though Tarquin had already expired, he, under pretense of discharging the duty of
another, strengthened his own interest. Then at length,
the matter being made public, and lamentations being raised

in the palace, Servius, supported by a strong guard, took possession of the kingdom by the consent of the Senate, being the first who did so without the orders of the people. The children of Ancus, the instruments of their villainy having been already seized, as soon as it was announced that the king still lived, and that the power of Servius was so great, had already gone into exile to Suessa Pometia.

42. And now Servius began to strengthen his power, not more by public than by private[1] measures; and, lest the feelings of the children of Tarquin might be the same towards himself as those of the children of Ancus had been towards Tarquin, he unites his two daughters in marriage, to the young princes, the Tarquinii, Lucius and Aruns. Nor yet did he break through the inevitable decrees of fate by human measures, so that envy of the sovereign power should not produce general treachery and animosity even among the members of his own family. Very opportunely for maintaining the tranquillity of the present state, a war was commenced with the Veientes (for the truce had now expired[2]) and with the other Etrurians. In that war both the valor and good-fortune of Tullius were conspicuous, and he returned to Rome, after routing a great army of the enemy, now unquestionably king, whether he tried the dispositions of the fathers or the people. He then sets about a work of peace of the utmost importance; that, as Numa had been the author of religious institutions, so posterity might celebrate Servius as the founder of all distinction among the

[1] By *public—private.* The "public" were the steps taken by Servius to establish his political ascendency, while the "private" refer to those intended to strengthen his family connections.

[2] *The truce had now expired.* If the truce concluded with them by Romulus be here meant, it was long since expired, since about 140 years had now elapsed. It is probable, however, that it was renewed in the reign of Tullius.

4 *

members of the state, and of those orders by which a limi-
tation is established between the degrees of rank and fortune.   For he instituted the census — a most salutary measure for an empire destined to become so great, according to
which the services of war and peace were to be performed,
not by every person (indiscriminately), as formerly, but in
proportion to the amount of property.   Then he formed,
according to the census, the classes and centuries, and the
arrangement as it now exists eminently suited either to
peace or war.

43. Of those who had an estate of a hundred thousand
asses or more, he made eighty centuries, forty of seniors and
forty of juniors.   All these were called the first class : the
seniors were to be in readiness to guard the city, the juniors to carry on war abroad.   The arms enjoined them were
a helmet, a round shield, greaves, and a coat of mail, all of
brass ; these were for the defense of their body ; their
weapons of offense were a spear and a sword.   To this class
were added two centuries of mechanics, who were to serve
without arms ; the duty imposed upon them was to carry the
military engines.   The second class comprehended all whose
estate was from seventy-five to a hundred thousand asses ;
and of these, seniors and juniors, twenty centuries were enrolled.   The arms enjoined them were a buckler instead of a
shield, and except a coat of mail, all the rest were the same.
He appointed the property of the third class to amount to
fifty thousand asses ; the number of centuries was the same,
and formed with the same distinction of age ; nor was there
any change in their arms, only greaves were taken from
them.   In the fourth class, the property was twenty-five
thousand asses, the same number of centuries was formed :
the arms were changed, nothing was given them but a spear
and a long javelin.   The fifth class was increased, thirty

centuries were formed ; these carried slings and stones for throwing. Among them were reckoned the horn-blowers and the trumpeters, distributed into three centuries. This whole class was rated at eleven thousand asses. Property lower than this comprehended all the rest of the citizens, and of them one century was made up which was exempted from serving in war. Having thus divided and armed the infantry, he levied twelve centuries of knights from among the chief men of the state. Likewise out of the three centuries appointed by Romulus he formed other six under the same names which they had received at their first institution. Ten thousand asses were given them out of the public revenue for the buying of horses, and widows were assigned them, who were to pay two thousand asses yearly for the support of the horses. All these burdens were taken off the poor and laid on the rich. Then an additional honor was conferred upon them ; for the suffrage was not now granted promiscuously to all, as it had been established by Romulus, and observed by his successors, to every man with the same privilege and the same right, but gradations were established, so that no one might seem excluded from the right of voting, and yet the whole power might reside in the chief men of the state. For the knights were first called, and then the eighty centuries of the first class ; and if they happened to differ, which was seldom the case, those of the second were called ; and they seldom ever descended so low as to come to the lowest class. Nor need we be surprised that the present regulation which now exists, since the tribes were increased to thirty-five, should not agree in the number of centuries of juniors and seniors with the amount instituted by Servius Tullius, they being now double of what they were at that time. For the city being divided into four parts, according to the regions and hills which were then inhabited, he called these divisions tribes, as I think, from the tribute.[1] For the method of levying taxes ratably according to the value of estates was also introduced by him; nor had these tribes any relation to the number and distribution of the centuries.

44. The census being now completed, which he had expedited by the terror of a law passed on those not rated, with threats of imprisonment and death, he issued a proclamation that all the Roman citizens, horse and foot, should attend at the dawn of day in the Campus Martius, each in his century. There he drew up his army, and performed a lustration of it by the sacrifices called suovetaurilia; and that was called the closing of the lustrum, because that was the conclusion of the census. Eighty thousand citizens are said to have been rated in that survey. Fabius Pictor, the oldest of our historians, adds that such was the number of those who were able to bear arms. To accommodate that number the city seemed to require enlargement. He adds two hills, the Quirinal and Viminal; then, in continuation, he enlarges the Esquiliæ, and takes up his own residence there, in order that respectability might attach to the place. He surrounds the city with a rampart, a moat, and a wall; thus he enlarges the Pomœrium. They who regard only the etymology of the word will have the Pomœrium to be a space of ground without the walls; but it is rather a space on each side the wall, which the Etrurians, in building cities, consecrated by augury, reaching to a certain extent both within and without in the direction they intended to raise the wall; so that the houses might not be joined to it on the inside, as they commonly are now, and also that there might be some space without left free from human occupa-

[1] Varro, de L. L. iv. 36, thinks, on the contrary, that *tributum* was so called, as being paid by the *tribes*.

tion. This space, which it was not lawful to till or inhabit, the Romans called the Pomœrium, not for its being without the wall, more than for the wall's being without it : and in enlarging the city, as far as the walls were intended to proceed outward, so far these consecrated limits were likewise extended.

45. The state being increased by the enlargement of the city, and every thing modelled at home and abroad for the exigencies both of peace and war, that the acquisition of power might not always depend on mere force of arms, he endeavored to extend his empire by policy, and at the same time to add some ornament to the city. The Temple of Diana at Ephesus was at that time in high renown ; fame represented it to have been built by all the states of Asia in common. When Servius, amidst some grandees of the Latins with whom he had taken pains to form connections of hospitality and friendship, extolled in high terms such concord and association of their gods, by frequently insisting on the same subject, he at length prevailed so far as that the Latin states agreed to build a temple to Diana at Rome,[1] in conjunction with the Roman people. This was an acknowledgement that Rome was the head of both nations, concerning which they had so often disputed in arms. Though that object seemed to have been left out of consideration by all the Latins, in consequence of the matter having been so often attempted unsuccessfully by arms, fortune seemed to present one of the Sabines with an opportunity of recovering the superiority to his country by his own address. A cow is said to have been calved to a certain person, the head of a family among the Sabines, of surprising size and beauty.

---

[1] *Temple of Diana.* Built on the summit of the Aventine Mount towards the Tiber. On its brazen pillar were engraved the laws of the treaty, and which were still extant in the time of Augustus.

Her horns, which were hung up in the porch of the Temple of Diana, remained for many ages, a monument of this wonder. The thing was looked upon as a prodigy, as it was, and the soothsayers declared that sovereignty would reside in that state of which a citizen should immolate this heifer to Diana. This prediction had also reached the ears of the high-priest of Diana. The Sabine, when he thought the proper time for offering the sacrifice was come, drove the cow to Rome, led her to the temple of that goddess, and set her before the altar. The Roman priest, struck with the uncommon size of the victim, so much celebrated by fame, thus accosted the Sabine: "What intendest thou to do, stranger?" says he. "Is it with impure hands to offer a sacrifice to Diana? Why dost not thou first wash thyself in running water? The Tiber runs along in the bottom of that valley." The stranger, being seized with a scruple of conscience, and desirous of having every thing done in due form, that the event might answer the prediction, from the temple went down to the Tiber. In the mean time the priest sacrificed the cow to Diana, which gave great satisfaction to the king and to the whole state.

46. Servius, though he had now acquired an indisputable right to the kingdom by long possession, yet as he heard that expressions were sometimes thrown out by young Tarquin, importing "That he held the crown without the consent of the people," having first secured their good will by dividing among them, man by man, the lands taken from their enemies, he ventured to propose the question to the people, whether they "chose and ordered that he should be king," and was declared king with such unanimity as had not been observed in the election of any of his predecessors. But this circumstance diminished not Tarquin's hope of obtaining the throne; nay, because he had observed that the

question of the distribution of land to the people[1] was carried against the will of the fathers, he felt so much the more satisfied that an opportunity was now presented to him of arraigning Servius before the fathers, and of increasing his own influence in the Senate, he being himself naturally of a fiery temper, and his wife, Tullia, at home stimulating his restless temper.   For the Roman palace also afforded an instance of tragic guilt; so that, through their disgust of kings, liberty might come more matured, and the throne which should be attained through crime might be the last. This L. Tarquinius (whether he was the son or grandson of Tarquinius Priscus is not clear; with the greater number of authorities, however, I would say his son[2]) had a brother, Aruns Tarquinius, a youth of a mild disposition.   To these two, as has been already stated, the two Tulliæ, daughters of the king, had been married, they also being of widely different tempers.   It had so happened, that the two violent dispositions were not united in marriage, through the good fortune, I suspect, of the Roman people, in order that the reign of Servius might be more protracted, and the morals of the state be firmly established.   The haughty Tullia was chagrined that there was no material in her husband either for ambition or bold daring.   Directing all her regard to the other Tarquinius, him she admired, him she called a man, and one truly descended of royal blood; she expressed her contempt of her sister, because, having got a man, she was deficient in the spirit becoming a woman.   Similarity of mind soon draws them together, as wickedness is in general most congenial to wickedness.   But the commencement

---

[1] This is noticed as the first trace of the Agrarian division by Niebuhr, i. p. 161.

[2] *His son.* Dionysius will have it that he was the grandson. See Nieb., i. p. 367.

of producing general confusion originated with the woman.
She, accustomed to the secret conversations of the other's
husband, refrained not from using the most contumelious
language of her husband to his brother, of her sister to (her
sister's) husband, and contended that it were better that she
herself were unmarried, and he single, than that they should
be matched unsuitably, so that they must languish away
through life by reason of the dastardly conduct of others.
If the gods had granted her the husband of whom she was
worthy, that she should soon see the crown in her own
house, which she now saw at her father's. She soon in-
spires the young man with her own daring notions. Aruns
Tarquinius and the younger Tullia, when they had, by im-'
mediate successive deaths, made their houses vacant for new
nuptials, are united in marriage, Servius rather not prohibit-
ing than approving the measure.

47. Then indeed the old age of Servius began to be every
day more disquieted, his reign to be more unhappy. For now
the woman looked from one crime to another, and suffered
not her husband to rest by night or by day, lest their past
murders might go for nothing. "That what she had wanted
was not a person whose wife she might be called, or one
with whom she might in silence live a slave ; what she had
wanted was one who would consider himself worthy of the
throne ; who would remember that he was the son of Tarquinius Priscus ; who would rather possess a kingdom than
hope for it. If you, to whom I consider myself married,
are such an one, I address you both as husband and king ;
but if not, our condition has been changed so far for the
worse, as in that person crime is associated with meanness.
Why not prepare yourself? It is not necessary for you, as
for your father, (coming here) from Corinth or Tarquinii,
to strive for foreign thrones. Your household and country's

gods, the image of your father, and the royal palace, and
the royal throne in that palace, constitute and call you king.
Or if you have too little spirit for this, why do you disappoint the nation? Why do you suffer yourself to be
looked up to as a prince? Get hence to Tarquinii or Corinth. Sink back again to your (original) race, more like
your brother than your father.'' By chiding him in these
and other terms, she spurs on the young man; nor can she
herself rest; (indignant) that, when Tanaquil, a foreign
woman, could achieve so great a project as to bestow two successive thrones on her husband, and then on her son-in-law,
she, sprung from royal blood, should have no weight in be-
stowing and taking away a kingdom. Tarquinius, driven on
by these frenzied instigations of the woman, began to go
round and solicit the patricians, especially those of the
younger families;[1] reminded them of his father's kindness,
and claimed a return for it; enticed the young men by presents; increased his interest, as well by making magnificent
promises on his own part as by inveighing against the king
at every opportunity. At length, as soon as the time seemed
convenient for accomplishing his object, he rushed into the
Forum, accompanied by a party of armed men; then, while
all were struck with dismay, seating himself on the throne
before the Senate-house, he ordered the fathers to be summoned to the Senate-house by the crier to attend King Tarquinius. They assembled immediately, some being already
prepared for the occasion, some through fear, lest their not
having come might prove detrimental to them, astounded at
the novelty and strangeness of the matter, and considering
that it was now all over with Servius. Then Tarquinius,

---

[1] *Younger families.* These had been brought into the Senate, as we
have seen, by Tarquinius Priscus, and consequently favored the Tarquinian interest. Nieb. i. p. 372.

commencing his invectives against his immediate ancestors:
"That a slave, and born of a slave, after the untimely death
of his parent, without an interregnum being adopted, as on
former occasions, without any comitia (being held), without
the suffrages of the people, or the sanction of the fathers,
he had taken possession of the kingdom as the gift of a
woman. That so born, so created king, ever a favorer of the
most degraded class, to which he himself belongs, through
a hatred of the high station of others, he had taken their
land from the leading men of the state and divided it among
the very meanest; that he had laid all the burdens, which
were formerly common, on the chief members of the com-
munity; that he had instituted the census, in order that the
fortune of the wealthier citizens might be conspicuous to
(excite) public envy, and that all was prepared whence he
might bestow largesses on the most needy whenever he might
please."

48. When Servius, aroused by the alarming announcement, came in during this harangue, immediately from the
porch of the Senate-house, he says, with a loud voice:
"What means this, Tarquin? by what audacity hast thou
dared to summon the fathers, while I am still alive? or to
sit on my throne?" To this, when he fiercely replied
"that he, the son of a king, occupied the throne of his
father, a much fitter successor to the throne than a slave;
that he (Servius) had insulted his masters full long enough
by his arbitrary shuffling," a shout arises from the partisans of both, and a rush of the people into the Senate-
house took place, and it became evident that whoever came
off victor would have the throne. Then Tarquin, necessity
itself now obliging him to have recourse to the last ex-
tremity, having much the advantage both in years and
strength, seizes Servius by the middle, and, having taken

him out of the Senate-house, throws him down the steps to
the bottom. He then returns to the Senate-house to assemble the Senate. The king's officers and attendants fly. He
himself, almost lifeless, when he was returning home with
his royal retinue frightened to death, and had arrived at the
top of the Cyprian Street, is slain by those who had been
sent by Tarquin, and had overtaken him in his flight. As
the act is not inconsistent with her other marked conduct, it
is believed to have been done by Tullia's advice. Certain
it is (for it is readily admitted), that driving into the Forum
in her chariot, and not abashed by the crowd of persons
there, she called her husband out of the Senate-house, and
was the first to style him king; and when, on being commanded by him to withdraw from such a tumult, she was returning home, and had arrived at the top of the Cyprian
Street, where Diana's temple lately was, as she was turning
to the right to the Orbian hill, in order to arrive at the Esquiline, the person who was driving, being terrified, stopped
and drew in the reins, and pointed out to his mistress the
murdered Servius as he lay. On this occasion a revolting
and inhuman crime is stated to have been committed, and
the place is a monument of it. They call it the Wicked
Street, where Tullia, frantic and urged on by the furies of
her sister and husband, is reported to have driven her chariot over her father's body, and to have carried a portion of
her father's body and blood to her own and her husband's
household gods, herself also being stained and sprinkled
with it; through whose vengeance results corresponding to
the wicked commencement of the reign were soon to follow.
Tullius reigned forty-four years, in such a manner that a
competition with him would prove difficult even for a good
and moderate successor. But this, also, has been an accession to his glory, that with him perished all just and legiti-

mate reigns. This authority, so mild and so moderate, yet, because it was vested in one, some say that he had it in contemplation to resign,[1] had not the wickedness of his family interfered with him while meditating the liberation of his country.

49. After this period Tarquin began his reign, whose actions procured him the surname of the Proud, for he refused his father in-law burial, alleging that even Romulus died without sepulture. He put to death the principal Senators, whom he suspected of having been in the interest of Servius. Then, conscious that the precedent of obtaining the crown by evil means might be adopted from him against himself, he surrounded his person with armed men, for he had no claim to the kingdom except force, inasmuch as he reigned without either the order of the people or the sanction of the Senate. To this was added (the fact) that, as he reposed no hope in the affection of his subjects, he found it necessary to secure his kingdom by terror; and in order to strike this into the greater number, he took cognizance of capital cases solely by himself without assessors; and under that pretext he had it in his power to put to death, banish, or fine, not only those who were suspected or hated, but those also from whom he could obtain nothing else but plunder. The number of the fathers more especially being thus diminished, he determined to elect none into the Senate, in order that the order might become contemptible by their very paucity, and that they might feel the less resentment at no business being transacted by them. For he was the first king who violated the custom derived from his predecessors of consulting the Senate on all subjects; he administered the public business by domestic counsels. War, peace, treaties, alliances, he

[1] *To resign.* Niebuhr is of opinion that what is said regarding the Commentaries of Servius Tullius, chap. 60, has reference to this.

contracted and dissolved with whomsoever he pleased, without the sanction of the people and Senate. The nation of the Latins in particular he wished to attach to him, so that by foreign influence also he might be more secure among his own subjects; and he contracted not only ties of hospitality, but affinities also, with their leading men. To Octavius Mamilius of Tusculum he gives his daughter in marriage (he was by far the most eminent of the Latin name, being descended, if we believe tradition, from Ulysses and the goddess Circe, and by this match he attaches to himself his numerous kinsmen and friends).

50. The influence of Tarquin among the chief men of the Latins was now considerable, when he issues an order that they should assemble on a certain day at the grove of Ferentina; that there was business about which he wished to confer with them touching their common interest. They assemble in great numbers at the break of day. Tarquinius himself observed the day indeed, but he came a little before sunset. Many matters were there canvassed in the meeting in various conversations. Turnus Herdonius, from Aricia, inveighed violently against Tarquin for his absence. "That it was no wonder the cognomen of Proud was given him at Rome;" for they now called him so secretly and in whispers, but still generally. "Could any thing be more proud than thus to trifle with the entire nation of the Latins? After their chiefs had been called at so great a distance from home, that he who summoned the meeting did not attend; that no doubt their patience was tried, in order that, if they submitted to the yoke, he may crush them when at his mercy. For to whom did it not plainly appear that he was aiming at sovereignty over the Latins? But if his own countrymen did well in intrusting it to him, or if it was intrusted, and not seized on by means of murder, that the

Latins also ought to intrust him (though not even so, inasmuch, as he was a foreigner). But if his own subjects are dissatisfied with him (seeing that they are butchered one upon another, driven into exile, and deprived of their property), what better prospects are held out to the Latins? If they follow his advice, that they would depart thence each to his own home, and take no more notice of the day of meeting than the person who appointed it." When this man, turbulent and daring, and one who had attained influence at home by these means, was pressing these and other observations having the same tendency, Tarquin came in. This put a conclusion to his harangue. All turned away from him to salute Tarquin, who, on silence being enjoined, being advised by those next to him to apologize for having come at that time, says that he had been chosen arbiter between a father and a son; that from his anxiety to reconcile them he had delayed; and because that circumstance had consumed that day, that on the morrow he would transact the business which he had determined on. They say that he did not make even that observation without a remark from Turnus: "That no controversy was shorter than one between a father and son, and that it might be decided in a few words—unless he submitted to his father, that he must prove unfortunate.

51. The Arician withdrew from the meeting, uttering these reflections against the Roman king. Tarquin, feeling the matter much more acutely than he appeared to do, immediately sets about planning the death of Turnus, in order that he might inspire into the Latins the same terror with which he had crushed the spirits of his own subjects at home; and because he could not be put to death openly, by virtue of his authority, he accomplished the ruin of this innocent man by bringing a false accusation against him.

By means of some Aricians of the opposite faction, he bribed
a servant of Turnus with gold, to suffer a great number of
swords to be introduced privately into his lodging.   When
this had been completed in the course of one night, Tarquin,
having summoned the chiefs of the Latins to him a little
before day, as if alarmed by some strange occurrence, says,
"that his delay of yesterday, having been occasioned, as it
were, by some providential care of the gods, had been the
means of preservation to him and them ; that it was told to
him that destruction was prepared by Turnus for him and
the chiefs of the Latins, that he alone might obtain the
government of the Latins.   That he was to have made the
attempt yesterday at the meeting ; that the matter was deferred, because the person who summoned the meeting was
absent, whom he chiefly aimed at.   That thence arose that
abuse of him for being absent, because he disappointed his
hopes by delaying.   That he had no doubt but, that if the
truth were told him, he would come at the break of day,
when the assembly met, attended with a band of conspirators, and with arms in his hands.   That it was said that a
great number of swords had been conveyed to his house.
Whether that be true or not, might be known immediately.
He requested that they would accompany him thence to
Turnus."   Both the daring temper of Turnus and his harangue of yesterday, and the delay of Tarquin, rendered the
matter suspicious, because it seemed possible that the murder might have been put off in consequence of it.   They
proceed then with minds inclined, indeed, to believe, yet
determined to consider every thing false unless the swords
were detected.   When they arrived there, Turnus is aroused
from sleep, and guards are placed around him ; and the servants, who, from affection to their master, were preparing
to use force, being secured, when the swords, which had

been concealed, were drawn out from all parts of the lodging, then indeed the whole matter appeared manifest, and chains were placed on Turnus; and forthwith a meeting of the Latins was summoned amidst great confusion. There on the swords being brought forward in the midst, such violent hatred arose against him, that, without being allowed a defense, by a novel mode of death—being thrown into the reservoir of the water of Ferentina, a hurdle[1] being placed over him, and stones being thrown into that—he was drowned.

52. Tarquin, having recalled the Latins to the meeting, and applauded those who had inflicted well-merited punishment on Turnus, as one convicted of parricide, by his attempting a change of government, spoke as follows : "That he could indeed proceed by a long-established right ; because, since all the Latins were sprung from Alba, they were included in that treaty by which the entire Alban nation, with their colonies, fell under the dominion of Rome, under Tullus. However, for the sake of the interest of all parties, he thought rather that that treaty should be renewed ; and that the Latins should, as participators, enjoy the prosperity of the Roman people, rather than that they should be constantly either apprehending or suffering the demolition of their town and the devastations of their lands, which they suffered formerly in the reign of Ancus, afterwards in the reign of his own father." The Latins were persuaded without any difficulty, though in that treaty the advantage lay on the side of Rome ; but they both saw that the chiefs of the Latin nation sided and concurred with the king, and Turnus was a recent instance of his danger to each, if he should make any opposition. Thus the treaty was renewed,

---

[1] *Hurdle*, a mode of punishment in use among the Carthaginians. See Tac. Germ. 12. Similar to the Greek κατατοντισμός.

and notice was given to the young men of the Latins that, according to the treaty, they should attend in considerable numbers in arms, on a certain day, at the grove of Ferentina. And when they assembled from all the states according to the edict of the Roman king, in order that they should neither have a general of their own nor a separate command, nor their own standards, he compounded companies of Latins and Romans, so as to make one out of two, and two out of one; the companies being thus doubled, he appointed centurions over them.

53. Nor was Tarquin, though a tyrannical prince in peace, a despicable general in war; nay, he would have equalled his predecessors in that art, had not his degeneracy[1] in other respects likewise detracted from his merit here. He began the war against the Volsci, which lasted two hundred years after his time, and took from them Suessa Pometia by storm; and when, by the sale of the spoils, he had amassed forty talents of silver and of gold, he designed such magnificence for a temple to Jupiter as should be worthy of the king of gods and men, of the Roman empire, and of the majesty of the place itself: for the building of this temple he set apart the money arising from the spoils. Soon after a war came upon him, more tedious than he expected, in which, having in vain, attempted to storm Gabii, a city in his neighborhood, when, being repulsed from the walls, all hopes of taking it by siege also was taken from him, he assailed it by fraud and stratagem, arts by no means Roman. For when, as if the war was laid aside, he pretended to be busily taken up with laying the foundation of the temple, and with his other works in the city, Sextus, the youngest of his three sons, according to concert, fled to Gabii, complaining of the in-

---

[1] *His degeneracy—degeneratum.* This use of the passive participle is of frequent occurrence in Livy.

5

human cruelty of his father, "that he had turned his tyranny from others against his own family, and was uneasy
at the number of his own children, intending to make the
same desolations in his own house which he had made in
the Senate, in order that he might leave behind him no issue nor heir to his kingdom.   That for his own part, as he
had escaped amidst the swords and other weapons of his
father, he was persuaded he could find no safety anywhere
but among the enemies of L. Tarquin.   And, that they
might not be led astray, that the war, which it is now pretended has been given up, still lies in reserve, and that he
would attack them when off their guard on the occurrence
of an opportunity.   But if there be no refuge for suppliants among them, that he would traverse all Latium, and
would apply to the Volscians, and Æquians, and Hernicians, until he should come to those who knew how to protect children from the impious and cruel persecution of
parents.   That perhaps he would find some ardor also to
take up arms and wage war against this proud king and his
haughty subjects."   As he seemed a person likely to go
farther onward, incensed with anger, if they paid him no
regard, he is received by the Gabians very kindly.   They
bid him not to be surprised if he were at last the same to his
children as he had been to his subjects and allies ; that he
would ultimately vent his rage on himself if other objects
failed him ; that his coming was very acceptable to them,
and they thought that it would come to pass that by his aid
the war would be transferred from the gates of Gabii to the
walls of Rome.

54. Upon this he was admitted into their public councils,
where, though with regard to other matters, he professed to
submit to the judgment of the old inhabitants of Gabii, to
whom they were better known, yet he every now and then

advised them to renew the war ; to that he pretended to a
superior knowledge, because he was well acquainted with
the strength of both nations and knew that the king's pride
was decidedly become hateful to his subjects, which not
even his own children could now endure.   As he thus by
degrees stirred up the nobles of the Gabians to renew the
war, went himself with the most active of their youth on
plundering parties and expeditions, and ill-grounded credit
was attached to all his words and actions, framed, as they
were, for deception, he is at length chosen general-in-
chief in the war.   There when, the people being still ignorant of what was really going on, several skirmishes with
the Romans took place, wherein the Gabians generally had
the advantage, then all the Gabians, from the highest to the
lowest, were firmly persuaded that Sextus Tarquinius had
been sent to them as their general by the special favor of
the gods.   By his exposing himself to fatigues and dangers,
and by his generosity in dividing the plunder, he was so
beloved by the soldiers that Tarquin the father had not
greater power at Rome than the son at Gabii.   When he saw
he had got sufficient strength collected to support him in
any undertaking, he sent one of his confidants to Rome to
ask his father what he wished him to do, seeing the gods had
granted him the sole management of all affairs at Gabii.   To
this courier no answer by word of mouth was given, because,
I suppose, he appeared of questionable fidelity.   The king
going into a garden of the palace, as it were, to consider of
the matter, followed by his son's messenger ; walking there
for some time in silence, he is said to have struck off the
heads of the tallest poppies with his staff.   The messenger,
wearied with demanding and waiting for an answer, returned
to Gabii, as if without having accomplished his object, and
told what he had said himself and what he had observed,

adding, "that Tarquin, either through passion, aversion to
him, or his innate pride, had not spoken a word." As soon
as it became evident to Sextus what his father wished and
what conduct he recommended by those silent intimations,
he put to death the most eminent men of the city, accusing
some of them to the people, and others who were exposed
by their own unpopularity. Many were executed publicly,
and some, against whom an impeachment was likely to
prove less specious, were secretly assassinated. Means of
escape were to some allowed, and others were banished, and
their estates, as well as the estates of those who were put to
death, publicly distributed. By the sweets of corruption,
plunder and private advantage resulting from these distri-
butions, the sense of the public calamities became extin-
guished in them, till the state of Gabii, destitute of counsel
and assistance, was delivered without a struggle into the
hands of the Roman king.

55. Tarquin, thus put in possession of Gabii, made peace
with the Æquians, and renewed the treaty with the Etrurians. Then he turned his thoughts to the business of the
city. The chief whereof was that of leaving behind him
the temple of Jupiter on the Tarpeian Mount, as a monument of his name and reign; [since posterity would remem-
ber] that of two Tarquinii, both kings, the father had vowed,
the son completed it. And that the area, excluding all other
forms of worship, might be entirely appropriated to Jupiter
and his temple, which was to be erected upon it, he resolved
to unhallow several small temples and chapels, which had
been vowed first by King Tatius, in the heat of the battle
against Romulus, and which he afterwards consecrated and
dedicated. In the very beginning of founding this work it
is said that the gods exerted their divinity to presage the
future greatness of this empire; for though the birds de-

clared for the unhallowing of all the other temples, they
did not admit of it with respect to that of Terminus. This
omen and augury were taken to import that Terminus's not
changing his residence, and being the only one of the gods
who was not called out of the places devoted to their worship, presaged the duration and stability of their empire.
This being deemed an omen of the perpetuity, there followed another portending the greatness of the empire. It
is reported that the head of a man, with the face entire,
appeared to the workmen when digging the foundation of
the temple. The sight of this phenomenon unequivocally
presaged that this temple should be the metropolis of the
.empire, and the head of the world; and so declared the
soothsayers, both those who were in the city, and those whom
they had sent for from Etruria to consult on this subject.
The king was encouraged to enlarge the expense; so that
the spoils of Pometia, which had been destined to complete
the work, scarcely sufficed for laying the foundation. On
this account I am more inclined to believe Fabius Pictor,
besides his being the more ancient historian, that there were
only forty talents, than Piso, who says that forty thousand
pounds' weight of silver were set apart for that purpose—a
sum of money neither to be expected from the spoils of any
one city in those times, and one that would more than suf-
fice for the foundation of any structure, even though exhibiting the magnificence of modern structures.

56. Tarquin, intent upon finishing this temple, having
sent for workmen from all parts of Etruria, employed on it
not only the public money, but the manual labor of the
people; and when this labor, by no means inconsiderable in
itself, was added to their military service, still the people
murmured less at their building the temples of the gods
with their own hands; they were afterwards transferred to

other works, which, while less in show, (required) still greater toil : such as the erecting benches in the circus, and conducting under ground the principal sewer,[1] the receptacle of all the filth of the city ; to which two works even modern splendor can scarcely produce anything equal. The people having been employed in these works—because he both considered that such a multitude was a burden to the city when there was no employment for them, and further, he was anxious that the frontiers of the empire should be more extensively occupied by sending colonists—he sent colonists to Signia and Circeii, to serve as defensive barriers hereafter to the city by land and sea. While he was thus employed a frightful prodigy appeared to him. A serpent sliding out of a wooden pillar, after causing dismay and a run into the palace, not so much struck the king's heart with sudden terror as filled him with anxious solicitude. Accordingly, when Etrurian soothsayers only were employed for public prodigies, terrified at this, as it were, domestic apparition, he determined on sending persons to Delphos to the most celebrated oracle in the world ; and not venturing to intrust the responses of the oracle to any other person, he dispatched his two sons to Greece through lands unknown at that time, and seas still more so. Titus and Aruns were the two who went. To them were added, as a companion, L. Junius Brutus, the son of Tarquinia, sister to the king, a youth of an entirely different quality of mind from that the disguise of which he had assumed. Brutus, on hearing that the chief men of the city, and among others his own brother, had been put to death by his uncle, resolved to leave nothing in his intellects that might be dreaded by the king, nor any

---

[1] *The principal sewer—the cloaca maxima.* This is attributed to Tarquinius Priscus by several writers. Dio. iii. 67, states that it was he commenced it. See Plin. H. N. xxxvi. Nieb. i. p. 385.

thing in his fortune to be coveted, and thus to be secure in contempt, where there was but little protection in justice. Therefore, designedly fashioning himself to the semblance of foolishness, after he suffered himself and his whole estate to become a prey to the king, he did not refuse to take even the surname of Brutus, that, concealed under the cover of such a cognomen, that genius that was to liberate the Roman people might await its proper time.   He, being brought to Delphos by the Tarquinii rather as a subject of sport than as a companion, is said to have brought with him, as an offering to Apollo, a golden rod, inclosed in a staff of cornelwood hollowed out for the purpose, a mystical emblem of his own mind.   When they arrived there, their father's commission being executed, a desire seized the young men of inquiring on which of them the sovereignty of Rome should devolve.   They say that a voice was returned from the bottom of the cave : " Young men, whichever of you shall first kiss his mother shall enjoy the sovereign power at Rome."   The Tarquinii order the matter to be kept secret with the utmost care, that Sextus, who had been left behind at Rome, might be ignorant of the response, and have no share in the kingdom ; they cast lots among themselves as to which of them should first kiss his mother after they had returned to Rome.   Brutus, thinking that the Pythian response had another meaning, as if he had stumbled and fallen, touched the ground with his lips—she being, forsooth, the common mother of all mankind.   After this they all returned to Rome, where preparations were being made with the greatest vigor for a war against the Rutulians.

57. The Rutulians, a nation very wealthy, considering the country and age they lived in, were at that time in possession of Ardea.   Their riches gave occasion to the war ;

for the king of the Romans, being exhausted of money by the magnificence of his public works, was desirous both to enrich himself, and by a large booty to soothe the minds of his subjects, who, besides other instances of his tyranny, were incensed against his government, because they were indignant that they had been kept so long a time by the king in the employments of mechanics, and in labor fit for slaves.   An attempt was made to take Ardea by storm; when that did not succeed, the enemy began to be distressed by a blockade, and by works raised around them.   As it commonly happens in standing camps, the war being rather tedious than violent, furloughs were easily obtained, more so by the officers, however, than the common soldiers.   The young princes sometimes spent their leisure hours in feasting and entertainments.   One day as they were drinking in the tent of Sextus Tarquin, where Collatinus Tarquinius, the son of Egerius, was also at supper, mention was made of wives.   Every one commended his own in an extravagant manner, till a dispute arising about it, Collatinus said: "There was no occasion for words, that it might be known in a few hours how far his Lucretia excelled all the rest. If, then," added he, "we have any share of the vigor of youth, let us mount our horses and examine the behavior of our wives; that must be most satisfactory to every one, which shall meet his eyes on the unexpected arrival of the husband."   They were heated with wine: "Come on, then," say all.   They immediately galloped to Rome, where they arrived in the dusk of the evening.   From thence they went to Collatia, where they find Lucretia, not like the king's daughters-in-law, whom they had seen spending their time in luxurious entertainments with their equals, but, though at an advanced time of night, employed at her wool, sitting in the middle of the house amidst her maids working around

her. The merit of the contest regarding the ladies was
assigned to Lucretia. Her husband on his arrival, and the
Tarquinii, were kindly received ; the husband, proud of his
victory, gives the young princes a polite invitation. There
the villanous passion for violating Lucretia by force seizes
Sextus Tarquin ; both her beauty and her approved purity
act as incentives. And then, after this youthful frolic of
the night, they return to the camp.

58. A few days after, without the knowledge of Collatinus, Sextus came to Collatia with one attendant only; where,
being kindly received by them, as not being aware of his
intention, after he had been conducted after supper into the
guests' chamber, burning with passion, when every thing
around seemed sufficiently secure, and all fast asleep, he
comes to Lucretia, as she lay asleep, with a naked sword,
and with his left hand pressing down the woman's breast,
he says: "Be silent, Lucretia; I am Sextus Tarquin; I have
a sword in my hand; you shall die, if you utter a word."
When, awaking terrified from sleep, the woman beheld no
aid, impending death nigh at hand; then Tarquin acknowl-
edged his passion, entreated, mixed threats with entreaties,
tried the female's mind in every possible way. When he
saw her inflexible, and that she was not moved even by the
terror of death, he added to terror the threat of dishonor:
he says that he will lay a murdered slave naked by her side
when dead, so that she may be said to have been slain in
infamous adultery. When by the terror of this disgrace his
lust, as it were victorious, had overcome her inflexible
chastity, and Tarquin had departed, exulting in having
triumphed over a lady's honor, Lucretia, in melancholy
distress at so dreadful a misfortune, dispatches the same
messenger to Rome to her father, and to Ardea to her husband, that they would come each with one trusty friend;

5 *

that it was necessary to do so, and that quickly.[1] Sp. Lucretius comes with P. Valerius, the son of Volesus, Collatinus with L. Junius Brutus, with whom, as he was returning to Rome, he happened to be met by his wife's messenger. They find Lucretia sitting in her chamber in sorrowful dejection. On the arrival of her friends the tears burst from her eyes; and to her husband, on his inquiry "whether all was right," she says, "By no means, for what can be right with a woman who has lost her honor? The traces of another man are on your bed, Collatinus. But the body only has been violated, the mind is guiltless; death shall be my witness. But give me your right hands, and your honor, that the adulterer shall not come off unpunished. It is Sextus Tarquin who, an enemy in the guise of a guest, has borne away hence a triumph fatal to me and to himself, if you are men." They all pledge their honor; they attempt to console her, distracted as she was in mind, by turning away the guilt from her, constrained by force, on the perpetrator of the crime; that it is the mind sins, not the body; and that where intention was wanting guilt could not be. "It is for you to see," says she, "what is due to him. As for me, though I acquit myself of guilt, from punishment I do not discharge myself; nor shall any woman survive her dishonor pleading the example of Lucretia." The knife, which she kept concealed beneath her garment, she plunges into her heart, and falling forward on the wound, she dropped down expiring. The husband and father shriek aloud.

59. Brutus, while they were overpowered with grief, having drawn the knife out of the wound, and holding it up before him reeking with blood, said: "By this blood, most

---

[1] *To do so, and that quickly*—a use of the participles *facto* and *maturate* similar to that already noticed in chap. 53, *degeneratum*.

pure before the pollution of royal villainy, I swear, and I
call you, O gods, to witness my oath, that I shall pursue
Lucius Tarquin the Proud, his wicked wife, and all their
race, with fire, sword, and all other means in my power;
nor shall I ever suffer them or any other to reign at Rome."
Then he gave the knife to Collatinus, and after him to Lucretius and Valerius, who were surprised at such extraordinary mind in the breast of Brutus.   However, they all take
the oath as they were directed, and, converting their sorrow
into rage, follow Brutus as their leader, who from that time
ceased not to solicit them to abolish the regal power.   They
carry Lucretia's body from her own house and convey it
into the Forum, and assemble a number of persons, by the
strangeness and atrocity of the extraordinary occurrence, as
usually happens.   They complain, each for himself, of the
royal villainy and violence.   Both the grief of the father
moves them, as also Brutus, the reprover of their tears and
unavailing complaints, and their adviser to take up arms
against those who dared to treat them as enemies, as would
become men and Romans.   Each most spirited of the youth
voluntarily presents himself in arms; the rest of the youth
follow also.   From thence, after leaving an adequate garrison at the gates at Collatia, and having appointed sentinels,
so that no one might give intelligence of the disturbance to
the king's party, the rest set out for Rome in arms under
the conduct of Brutus.   When they arrived there, the
armed multitude cause panic and confusion wherever they
go.   Again, when they see the principal men of the state
placing themselves at their head, they think that, whatever
it may be, it was not without good reason.   Nor does the
heinousness of the circumstance excite less violent emotions
at Rome than it had done at Collatia; accordingly they run
from all parts of the city into the Forum, whither when they

came, the public crier summoned them to attend the tribune
of the celeres, with which office Brutus happened to be at
that time vested.   There a harangue was delivered by him,
by no means of that feeling and capacity which had been
counterfeited up to that day, concerning the violence and
lust of Sextus Tarquin, the horrid violation of Lucretia,
and her lamentable death, the bereavement of Tricipitinus,
to whom the cause of his daughter's death was more exasperating and deplorable than the death itself.   To this was
added the haughty insolence of the king himself, and the
sufferings and toils of the people, buried in the earth in
cleansing sinks and sewers; that the Romans, the conquerors
of all the surrounding states, instead of warriors had become laborers and stone-cutters.   The unnatural murder of
King Servius Tullius was dwelt on, and his daughter's driving over the body of her father in her impious chariot, and
the gods who avenge parents were invoked by him.   By
stating these and other, I suppose, more exasperating circumstances, which though by no means easily detailed by
writers, the heinousness of the case suggested at the time,
he persuaded the multitude, already incensed, to deprive
the king of his authority, and to order the banishment of
L. Tarquin, with his wife and children.   He himself, having selected and armed some of the young men, who readily
gave in their names, set out for Ardea to the camp, to excite
the army against the king: the command in the city he
leaves to Lucretius, who had been already appointed prefect
of the city by the king.   During this tumult Tullia fled
from her house, both men and women, cursing her wherever
she went, and invoking on her the furies, the avengers of
parents.

  60. News of these transactions having reached the camp,
when the king, alarmed at this sudden revolution, was going

to Rome to quell the commotions, Brutus, for he had notice of his approach, turned out of the way, that he might not meet him; and much about the same time Brutus and Tarquin arrived by different routes, the one at Ardea, the other at Rome.   The gates were shut against Tarquin, and an act of banishment passed against him; the deliverer of the state the camp received with great joy, and the king's sons were expelled.   Two of them followed their father, and went into banishment to Cære, a city of Etruria.   Sextus Tarquin, having gone to Gabii, as to his own kingdom, was slain by the avengers of the old feuds, which he had raised against himself by his rapines and murders.   Lucius Tarquin the Proud reigned twenty-five years: the regal form of government continued from the building of the city to this period of its deliverance, two hundred and forty-four years.   Two consuls, viz., Lucius Junius Brutus and Lucius Tarquinius Collatinus, were elected by the prefect of the city at the comitia by centuries, according to the commentaries of Servius Tullius.

BOOK II.

Brutus binds the people by oath never to suffer any king to reign at Rome; obliges Tarquinius Collatinus, his colleague, to resign the consulship, and leave the state; beheads some young noblemen, and among the rest his own and his sister's sons, for a conspiracy to receive the kings into the city. In a war against the Veientians and Tarquiniensians, he engages in single combat with Aruns, the son of Tarquin the Proud, and expires at the same time with his adversary. The ladies mourn for him a whole year. The Capitol dedicated. Porsena, king of Clusium, undertakes a war in favor of the Tarquins. Bravery of Horatius Cocles and of Mucius. Porsena concludes a peace on the receipt of hostages. Conduct of Clælia. Ap. Claudius removes from the country of the Sabines to Rome; for this reason the Claudian tribe is added to the former number, which by this means are increased to twenty-one. A. Posthumius the dictator defeats at the Lake Regillus Tarquin the Proud, making war upon the Romans with an army of Latins. Secession of the Commons to the Sacred Mount; brought back by Menenius Agrippa. Five tribunes of the people created. Corioli taken by C. Martius; from that he is surnamed Coriolanus. Banishment and subsequent conduct of C. M. Coriolanus. The Agrarian law first made. Sp. Cassius condemned and put to death. Oppia, a vestal virgin, buried alive for incontinence. The Fabian family undertake to carry on that war at their own cost and hazard, against the Veientians, and for that purpose send out three hundred and six men in arms, who were all cut off. Ap. Claudius the consul decimates his army because he had been unsuccessful in the war with the Veientians, by their refusing to obey orders. An account of the wars with the Volscians, Æquians, and Veientians, and the contests of the fathers with the commons.

1. THE affairs, civil and military, of the Roman people, henceforward free, their annual magistrates, and the sovereignty of the laws, more powerful than that of men, I

shall now detail. The haughty insolence of the late king
had caused this liberty to be the more welcome ; for the
former kings reigned in such a manner that they all in succession might be not undeservedly set down as founders of
the parts, at least of the city, which they added as new residences for the population augmented by themselves. Nor
is there a doubt but that the very same Brutus who earned
so much glory for expelling this haughty monarch would
have done so to the greatest injury of the public weal, if,
through an over-hasty desire of liberty, he had wrested the
kingdom from any of the preceding kings. For what would
have been the consequence if that rabble of shepherds and
strangers, fugitives from their own countries, having, under
the protection of an inviolable asylum, found liberty, or at
least impunity, uncontrolled by the dread of regal authority,
had begun to be distracted by tribunician storms, and to engage in contests with the fathers in a strange city, before the
pledges of wives and children, and love of the very soil, to
which it requires a length of time to become habituated,
had united their affections. Their affairs, not yet matured,
would have been destroyed by discord, which the tranquil
moderation of the government so cherished, and by proper
nourishment brought to such perfection, that their strength
being now developed, they were able to produce the whole-
some fruits of liberty. But the origin of liberty you may
date from this period, rather because the consular authority
was made annual, than that any diminution was made from
the kingly prerogative. The first consuls had all their privileges and ensigns of authority, only care was taken that the
terror might not appear doubled, by both having the fasces
at the same time. Brutus was, with the consent of his colleague, first attended by the fasces, who had not been a more
zealous assertor of liberty than he was afterwards its guar-

dian.   First of all he bound over the people, while still enraptured with their newly-acquired liberty, by an oath that
they would suffer no one to be king in Rome, lest afterwards
they might be perverted by the importunities or bribes of the
royal family.   Next in order, that the fullness of the house
might produce more of strength in the Senate, he filled up
the number of the Senators, diminished by the king's murders, to the amount of three hundred, having elected the
principal men of the equestrian rank ; and from thence it is
said the custom was derived of summoning into the Senate
both those who were patres and those who were conscripti.[1]
Forsooth they styled those who were elected into the new
Senate conscripti.   It is wonderful how much that contributed to the concord of the state, and to attach the affection
of the commons to the patricians.

2. Then attention was paid to religious matters, and as
some part of the public worship had been performed by the
kings in person, that they might not be missed in any respect, they elect a king of the sacrifices.   This office they
made subject to the pontiff, that honor being added to the
name might be no infringement on their liberty, which was
now their principal care.   And I know not whether by fenc-
ing it on every side to excess, even in the most trivial matters, they may not have exceeded bounds.   For, when there
was nothing else to offend, the name of one of the consuls
became an object of dislike to the state.   "That the Tarquinii had been too much habituated to sovereignty ; Priscus
first commenced ; that Servius Tullus reigned next ; that,
though an interval thus intervened, that Tarquinius Superbus, not losing sight of the kingdom as the property of
another, had reclaimed it by crime and violence as the

---

[1] All were called *Patres conscripti.*   Scil. Patres et Conscripti, the
conjunction being omitted. Nieb. L p. 517.

hereditary right of his family.   That Superbus being expelled, the government was in the hands of Collatinus ; that
the Tarquinii knew not how to live in a private station—
the name pleased them not ; that it was dangerous to liberty."   Such discourses were at first gradually circulated
through the entire state by persons sounding their dispositions ; and the people, now excited by jealousy, Brutus con-
venes to a meeting.   There, first of all, he recites the people's oath : " That they would suffer no one to be king, nor
anything to be in Rome whence danger might result to liberty.   That it ought to be maintained with all their might,
and nothing that could tend that way ought to be over-
looked ; he said it with reluctance, for the sake of the individual ; and would not say it, did not his affection for the
commonwealth predominate ; that the people of Rome do
not believe that entire liberty has been recovered ; that the
regal family, the regal name was not only in the state but
even in the government ; that was unfavorable, that was injurious to liberty.   Do you, L. Tarquinius," says he, "do
you, of your own accord, remove this apprehension.   We
remember, we own it, you expelled the royal family ; complete your kindness ; take hence the royal name—your
property your fellow-citizens shall not only restore you, by
my advice, but if anything is wanting they will generously
supply.   Depart in amity.   Relieve the state from a dread
which is perhaps groundless.   So firmly are they persuaded
in mind that only with the Tarquinian race will kingly
power depart hence."   Amazement at so extraordinary and
sudden an occurrence at first impeded the consul's utterance :
then, when he was commencing to speak, the chief men of
the state stand around him, and by many importunities urge
the same request.   Others, indeed, had less weight with him.
After Sp. Lucretius, superior in age and rank, his father-

in-law besides began to try various methods, by entreating and advising alternately, that he would suffer himself to be prevailed on by the general feeling of the state, the consul, apprehending lest hereafter these same things might befall him, when again in a private station, together with loss of property and other additional disgrace, he resigned his consulship ; and removing all his effects to Lavinium, he withdrew from the state.[1] Brutus, according to a decree of the Senate, proposed to the people that all the family of the Tarquins should be banished from Rome ; and in an assembly by centuries he elected P. Valerius, with whose assistance he had expelled the kings, for his colleague.

3. Though nobody doubted that a war was impending from the Tarquins, yet it broke out later than was universally expected ; but liberty was well-nigh lost by treachery and fraud, a thing they had never apprehended. There were among the Roman youth several young men of no mean families, who, during the regal government, had pursued their pleasures without any restraint, being of the same age with, and companions of, the young Tarquins, and accustomed to live in princely style. Longing for that licentiousness, now that the privileges of all were equalized, they complained that the liberty of others has been converted to their slavery : "that a king was a human being, from whom you can obtain, where right or where wrong may be necessary ; that there was room for favor and for kindness ; that he could be angry and could forgive ; that he knew the difference between a friend and an enemy ; that laws were a deaf, inexorable thing, more beneficial and advantageous for the poor than the rich ; that they allowed of no relaxa-

---

[1] Collatinus is supposed to have earned the odium of the people, and his consequent expulsion from Rome, by his endeavors to save his nephews, the Aquilii, from punishment.

tion or indulgence if you transgress bounds ; that it was a perilous state, amidst so many human errors, to live solely by one's integrity." While their minds were already thus discontented of their own accord, ambassadors from the royal family came unexpectedly, demanding restitution of their effects merely, without any mention of return. After their application was heard in the Senate, the deliberation on it lasted for several days, (fearing) lest the non-restitution might be a pretext for war, and the restitution a fund and assistance for war. In the mean time the ambassadors were planning different schemes ; openly demanding the property, they secretly concerted measures for recovering the throne, and soliciting them, as if for the object which appeared to be under consideration, they sound their feelings ; to those by whom their proposals were favorably received they give letters from the Tarquins and confer with them about admitting the royal family into the city secretly by night.

4. The matter was first intrusted to brothers of the name of Vitellii and those of the name of Aquilii. A sister of the Vitellii had been married to Brutus the consul, and the issue of that marriage were young men, Titus and Tiberius ; these also their uncles admit into a participation of the plot ; several young noblemen also were taken in as associates, the memory of whose names has been lost from distance of time. In the mean time, when that opinion had prevailed in the Senate which recommended the giving back of the property, and the ambassadors made use of this as a pretext for delay in the city, because they had obtained from the consuls time to procure modes of conveyance by which they might convey away the effects of the royal family ; all this time they spend in consulting with the conspirators, and by pressing, they succeed in having letters

given to them for the Tarquins. For otherwise how were
they to believe that the accounts brought by the ambassadors on matters of such importance were not idle? The
letters, given to be a pledge of their sincerity, discovered the
plot; for when, the day before the ambassadors set out to
the Tarquins, they had supped by chance at the house of
the Vitellii, and the conspirators there in private discoursed
much together concerning their new design, as is natural,
one of the slaves, who had already perceived what was going
on, overheard their conversation, but waited for the occasion when the letters should be given to the ambassadors,
the detection of which would prove thé transaction; when
he perceived that they were given, he laid the whole affair
before the consuls. The consuls, having left their home to
seize the ambassadors and conspirators, crushed the whole
affair without any tumult; particular care being taken of
the letters lest they should escape them. The traitors being immediately thrown into chains, a little doubt was entertained respecting the ambassadors, and, though they deserved to be considered as enemies, the law of nations
however prevailed.

5. The question concerning the restitution of the tyrants'
effects, which the Senate had formerly voted, came again
under consideration. The fathers, fired with indignation,
expressly forbade them either to be restored or confiscated.
They were given to be rifled by the people, that, after being
made participators in the royal plunder, they might lose
forever all hopes of a reconciliation with the Tarquins. A
field belonging to them, which lay between the city and the
Tiber, having been consecrated to Mars, has been called the
Campus Martius. It happened that there was a crop of
corn upon it ready to be cut down, which produce of the
field, as they thought it unlawful to use after it was reaped,

a great number of men carried the corn and straw in baskets
and threw them into the Tiber, which then flowed with
shallow water, as is usual in the heat of summer ; that thus
the heaps of corn, as it stuck in the shallows, became settled when covered over with mud ; by these and the afflux
of other things, which the river happened to bring thither,
an island was formed by degrees.   Afterwards I believe that
mounds were added, and that aid was afforded by art, that
a surface so well raised might be firm enough for sustaining
temples and porticoes.   After plundering the tyrants' effects,
the traitors were condemned and capital punishment inflicted.   Their punishment was the more remarkable, because the consulship imposed on the father the office of
punishing his own children, and him who should have been
removed as a spectator fortune assigned as the person to
exact the punishment.   Young men of the highest quality
stood tied to a stake ; but the consul's sons attracted the eyes
of all the spectators from the rest of the criminals, as from
persons unknown ; nor did the people pity them more, on
account of the severity of the punishment, than the horrid
crime by which they had deserved it.   "That they, in that
year particularly, should have brought themselves to betray
into the hands of Tarquin, formerly a proud tyrant, and
now an exasperated exile, their country just delivered, their
father its deliverer, the consulate which took its rise from
the family of the Junii, the fathers, the people, and whatever belonged either to the gods or the citizens of Rome." [1]
The consuls seated themselves in their tribunal, and the
lictors, being dispatched to inflict punishment, strip them
naked, beat them with rods, and strike off their heads.

[1] Niebuhr will have it that Brutus punished his children by his
authority as a father, and that there was no appeal to the people
from the father. See Nieb. i. p. 488.

While during all this time the father, his looks and his countenance, presented a touching spectacle,[1] the feelings of the father bursting forth occasionally during the office of superintending the public execution. Next after the punishment of the guilty, that there might be a striking example in either way for the prevention of crime, a sum of money was granted out of the treasury as a reward to the discoverer; liberty also and the rights of citizenship were granted him. He is said to have been the first person made free by the Vindicta; some think even that the term vindicta is derived from him. After him it was observed as a rule that those who were set free in this manner were supposed to be admitted to the rights of Roman citizens.[2]

6. On these things being announced to him as they had occurred, Tarquin, inflamed not only with grief for the frustration of such great hopes, but with hatred and resentment also, when he saw that the way was blocked up against stratagem, considering that he should have recourse to war openly, went round as a suppliant to the cities of Etruria, "that they should not suffer him, sprung from themselves, of the same blood, exiled and in want, lately in possession of so great a kingdom, to perish before their eyes, with the

[1] *Animo patris*, the strength of his mind, though that of a father, being even more conspicuous, etc. So Drakenborch understands the passage—this sternness of mind, he says, though he was their father, was a more remarkable spectacle than his stern countenance. This character of Brutus, as inferrible from the words thus interpreted, coincides with that given of him by Dionysius and others. I prefer understanding the passage with Crevier, scil. symptoms of paternal affection to his children displaying themselves during the discharge of his duty in superintending the public punishment inflicted on them.

[2] Previously, by the institution of Servius, only such manumitted slaves were admitted to the rights of citizenship as were registered by their masters in the census.

young men his sons. That others had been invited to Rome from foreign lands to the throne; that he, a king, extending the Roman empire by his arms, was driven out by those nearest to him by a villainous conspiracy; that they had by violence divided the parts among themselves, because no one individual among them was deemed sufficiently deserving of the kingdom; that they had given up his effects to the people to be pillaged by them, that no one might be free from that guilt. That he was desirous to recover his country and his kingdom, and to punish his ungrateful subjects. That they should bring succor and aid him; that they might also revenge the injuries done to them of old, their legions so often slaughtered, their land taken from them." These arguments prevailed on the people of Veii, and with menaces they declare that now at least, under the conduct of a Roman general, their former disgrace should be wiped off, and what they had lost in war should be recovered. His name and relation to them induced the people of Tarquinii to take part with him; it seemed an honor that their countrymen should reign at Rome. Therefore the two armies of these two states followed Tarquin in order to recover his kingdom, and to take vengeance upon the Romans. When they entered the Roman territories, the consuls marched to meet them. Valerius led up the foot in a square battalion, and Brutus marched before with his horse to reconnoitre (the enemy). Their cavalry likewise came up first; Aruns, Tarquin's son, commanded it; the king himself followed with the legions. Aruns, when he knew at a distance by the lictors that it was a consul, and on coming nigher discovered for certain that it was Brutus by his face, all inflamed with rage, he cried out: "There is the villain who has banished us from our native country! see how he rides in state adorned with the

ensigns of our dignity! now assist me, gods, the avengers
of kings." He put spurs to his horse and drove furiously
against the consul. Brutus perceived the attack made on
him ; as it was honorable in these days for the generals to
engage in combat, he eagerly offered himself to the combat.
They encountered one another with such furious animosity,
neither mindful of protecting his own person, provided he
could wound his adversary ; so that both, transfixed through
the buckler by the blow from the opposite direction, fell
lifeless from their horses, entangled together by the two
spears. The engagement between the rest of the horse
commenced at the same time, and soon after the foot came
up. There they fought with doubtful success, and as it were
with equal advantage, and the victory doubtful. The right
wings of both armies were victorious, and the left worsted.
The Veientians, accustomed to be discomfited by the Roman
soldiers, were routed and put to flight. The Tarquinienses,
who were a new enemy, not only stood their ground, but
even on their side obliged the Romans to give way.

7. After the issue of this battle, so great a terror seized
Tarquin and the Etrurians, that both the armies, the Veientian and Tarquinian, giving up the matter, as imprac-
ticable, departed to their respective homes. They annex
strange incidents to this battle—that in the silence of the
next night a loud voice was emitted from the Arsian wood ;
that it was believed to be the voice of Silvanus : these
words were spoken, "that more of the Etrurians by one[1]
had fallen in the battle ; that the Roman was victorious in
the war." Certainly the Romans departed thence as victors, the Etrurians as vanquished. For as soon as it was
light, and not one of the enemy was now to be seen, P.

---

[1] *Uno plus Tuscorum.* Ὡς ἐνὶ πλείους ἐν τη μὰχη τεθνήκασι Τυῤῥηῦῶν
ἠ Ῥωμαίων.

Valerius the consul collected the spoils, and returned thence
in triumph to Rome.   His colleague's funeral he celebrated
with all the magnificence then possible.   But a far greater
honor to his death was the public sorrow, singularly remarkable in this particular, that the matrons mourned him a year,[1]
as a parent, because he had been so vigorous an avenger of violated chastity.   Afterwards the consul who survived—so
changeable are the minds of the people from great popularity
—encountered not only jealousy, but suspicion, originating in
an atrocious charge.   Report represented that he aspired to
the crown, because he had not substituted a colleague in
the room of Brutus, and·was building a house on the summit of Mount Velia, that there would be an impregnable
fortress on an elevated and well-fortified place.   When
these things, thus circulated and believed, affected the consul's mind with indignation, having summoned the people
to an assembly, he mounts the rostrum, after lowering the
fasces.   It was a grateful sight to the multitude that the
insignia of authority were lowered to them, and that an ac-
knowledgment was made that the majesty and power of the
people were greater than that of the consul.   When they
were called to silence, Valerius highly extolled the good
fortune of his colleague, "who, after delivering his country,
had died vested with the supreme power, fighting bravely
in defence of the commonwealth, when his glory was in
its maturity, and not yet converted into jealousy.   That he
himself, having survived his glory, now remained as an object of accusation and calumny; that from the liberator of
his country he had fallen to the level of the Aquilii and
Vitellii.   Will no merit then, says he, ever be so tried and
approved by you as to be exempted from the attacks of suspicion?   Could I apprehend that myself, the bitterest enemy

---

[1] *A year*, scil. of ten months.

6

of kings, should fall under the charge of a desire of royalty?
Could I believe that, even though I dwelt in the very citadel
and the Capitol, that I could be dreaded by my fellow-citizens? Does my character among you depend on so mere a
trifle? Is my integrity so slightly founded, that it makes
more matter where I may be than what I may be? The
house of Publius Valerius shall not stand in the way of your
liberty, Romans; the Velian Mount shall be secure to you.
I will not only bring down my house into the plain, but I
will build it beneath the hill, that you may dwell above me,
a suspected citizen. Let those build on the Velian Mount
to whom liberty is more securely intrusted than to P. Valerius." Immediately all the material were brought down to
the foot of the Velian Mount, and the house was built at
the foot of the hill, where the Temple of Victory now stands.

8. After this laws were passed, which not only cleared
him of all suspicions of aiming at the regal power, but had
so contrary a tendency that they made him popular. From
thence he was surnamed Poplicola. Above all, the laws
regarding an appeal to the people against the magistrates,
and that devoting the life and property of any one who
should form a design of assuming regal authority, were
grateful to the people. And after he had passed these while
sole consul, so that the merit in them was exclusively his
own, he then held an assembly for the election of a new colleague. Sp. Lucretius was elected consul, who being very
old, and his strength being inadequate to discharge the consular duties, dies in a few days. M. Horatius Pulvillus was
substituted in the room of Lucretius. In some old writers I
find no mention of Lucretius as consul; they place Horatius
immediately after Brutus. I believe that, because no important event signalized his consulate, it has been unnoticed.
Jupiter's temple in the Capitol had not yet been dedicated;

the consuls Valerius and Horatius cast lots which should
dedicate it.   It fell by lot to Horatius.   Publicola departed
to the war of the Veientians.   The friends of Valerius were
more annoyed than they should have been, that the dedication of so celebrated a temple should be given to Horatius.[1]
Having endeavored by every means to prevent that, when -
all other attempts had been tried in vain, when the consul
was now holding the door-post during his offering of prayer
to the gods, they suddenly announce to him the shocking intelligence that his son was dead, and that his family being
defiled[1] he could not dedicate the temple.   Whether he did
not believe the fact, or possessed such great firmness of
mind, is neither handed down for certain, nor is a conjec-
ture easy.   Diverted from his purpose at this intelligence
in no other way than to order that the body should be
buried,[3] he goes through the prayer, and dedicates the
temple.   These were the transactions at home and abroad
the first year after the expulsion of the kings.   After this P.
Valerius, a second time, and Titus Lucretius, were elected
consuls.

9. By this time the Tarquins had fled to Lars[4] Porsena,
king of Clusium.   There, mixing advice with their entreaties, "They sometimes besought him not to suffer them,
who were descended from the Etrurians, and of the same
blood and name, to live in exile and poverty; at other times
they advised him not to let this commencing practice of

[1] The Horatii being of the *minores patres.*   Nieb. i. p. 533.

[2] *Funesta familia,* as having in it an unburied corpse.   Thus Mise-
nus, while unburied, *incestat funere classem.*   Virg. Æn. vi. 150.

[3] He here rejected the omen, Cic. i. 7. 14 ; auguria aut *oblativa* sunt,
quæ non poscuntur, aut *impetrativa,* quæ optata veniunt.   The latter
could not be rejected.

[4] *Lar.*   This is generally understood to have been a title of honor
equivalent to our term *Lord.*

expelling kings pass unpunished. That liberty has charms
enough in itself; and unless kings defend their crowns
with as much vigor as the people pursue their liberty, that
the highest must be reduced to a level with the lowest;
there will be nothing exalted, nothing distinguished above
the rest; and hence there must be an end of regal government, the most beautiful institution both among gods and
men." Porsena, thinking that it would be an honor to the
Tuscans both that there should be a king at Rome, and
especially one of the Etrurian nation, marched towards
Rome with a hostile army. Never before on any other
occasion did so great terror seize the Senate; so powerful
was the state of Clusium at the time, and so great the renown of Porsena. Nor did they only dread their enemies,
but even their own citizens, lest the common people,
through excess of fear, should, by receiving the Tarquins
into the city, accept peace even if purchased with slavery.
Many conciliatory concessions were therefore granted to the
people by the Senate during that period. Their attention,
in the first place, was directed to the markets, and persons
were sent, some to the Volscians, others to Cumæ, to buy up
corn. The privilege[1] of selling salt, also, because it was
farmed at a high rent, was all taken into the hands of government,[2] and withdrawn from private individuals; and the

[1] *Arbitrium* signifies not only the "privilege," but the "rent" paid
for such privilege, or right of monopoly.

[2] *Was all taken into the hands of government.* In my version of this
passage I have conformed to the emendation of the original first proposed by Gronovius, and admitted by Stroth and Bekker; scil. *in pub-
licum omne sumptum.* They did not let these salt-works by auction,
but took them into their own management, and carried them on by
means of persons employed to work on the public account. These
salt-works, first established at Ostia by Ancus, were, like other public
property, farmed out to the publicans. As they had a high rent to

people were freed from port-duties and taxes; that the rich,
who were adequate to bearing the burden, should contri-
bute; that the poor paid tax enough if they educated their
children.   This indulgent care of the fathers accordingly
kept the whole state in such concord amidst the subsequent severities in the siege and famine, that the highest
abhorred the name of king not more than the lowest; nor
was any single individual afterwards so popular by in-
triguing practices as the whole Senate then was by their
excellent government.

10. Some parts seemed secured by the walls, others by the
interposition of the Tiber.   The Sublician bridge well-nigh
afforded a passage to the enemy, had there not been one
man, Horatius Cocles (that defense the fortune of Rome had
on that day), who, happening to be posted on guard at the
bridge, when he saw the Janiculum taken by a sudden
assault, and that the enemy were pouring down from thence
in full speed, and that his own party, in terror and confusion,
were abandoning their arms and ranks, laying hold of them
one by one, standing in their way, and appealing to the faith
of gods and men, he declared, "That their flight would avail
them nothing if they deserted their post ; if they passed the
bridge and left it behind them, there would soon be more of
the enemy in the Palatium and Capitol than in the Janicu-·
lum ; for that reason he advised and charged them to demolish the bridge, by their sword, by fire, or by any means
whatever ; that he would stand the shock of the enemy as
far as could be done by one man."   He then advances to the

pay, the price of salt was raised in proportion; but now the patricians,
to curry favor with the plebeians, did not let the salt-pits to private
tenants, but kept them in the hands of public laborers, to collect all
the salt for the public use; and appointed salesmen to retail it to the
people at a cheaper rate.   See Stocker's ed.

first entrance of the bridge, and, being easily distinguished among those who showed their backs in retreating from the fight, facing about to engage the foe hand to hand, by his surprising bravery he terrified the enemy.   Two indeed a sense of shame kept with him, Sp. Lartius and T. Herminius, men eminent for their birth, and renowned for their gallant exploits.   With them he for a short time stood the first storm of the danger, and the severest brunt of the battle. But as they who demolished the bridge called upon them to retire, he obliged them also to withdraw to a place of safety on a small portion of the bridge still left.   Then casting his stern eyes round all the officers of the Etrurians in a threatening manner, he sometimes challenged them singly, sometimes reproached them all; "the slaves of haughty tyrants, who, regardless of their own freedom, came to oppress the liberty of others."   They hesitated for a considerable time, looking round one at the other, to commence the fight; · shame then put the army in motion, and a shout being raised, they hurl their weapons from all sides on their single adversary; and when they all stuck in the shield held before him, and he with no less obstinacy kept possession of the bridge with firm step, they now endeavored to thrust him down from it by one push, when at once the crash of the falling bridge, at the same time a shout of the Romans raised for joy at having completed their purpose, checked their ardor with sudden panic.   Then Cocles says : "Holy father Tiberinus, I pray that thou wouldst receive these arms, and this thy soldier, in thy propitious stream." Armed as he was, he leaped into the Tiber, and amidst showers of darts hurled on him, swam across safe to his party, having dared an act which is likely to obtain more fame than credit with posterity.   The state was grateful towards such valor; a statue was erected to him in the comitium, and as much land was given to him as he ploughed around in one day.   The zeal of private individuals also was conspicuous among the public honors.   For, amidst the great scarcity, each person contributed something to him according to his supply at home, depriving himself of his own support.

11. Porsena being repulsed in his first attempt, having changed his plans from a siege to a blockade, after he had placed a garrison in Janiculum, pitched his camp in the plain and on the banks of the Tiber.   Then sending for boats from all parts, both to guard the river, so as not to suffer any provision to be conveyed to Rome, and also to transport his soldiers across the river, to plunder different places as occasion required ; in a short time he so harassed the entire country round Rome, that not only every thing else from the country, but even their cattle, was driven into the city, and nobody durst venture thence without the gates. This liberty of action was granted to the Etrurians, not more through fear than from policy ; for Valerius, intent on an opportunity of falling unawares upon a number of them, and when straggling, a remiss avenger in trifling matters, reserved the weight of his vengeance for more important occasions.   Wherefore, to decoy the pillagers, he ordered his men to drive their cattle the next day out at the Esquiline gate, which was farthest from the enemy, presuming that they would get intelligence of it, because during the blockade and famine some slaves would turn traitors and desert.   Accordingly they were informed of it by a deserter, and parties more numerous than usual, in hopes of seizing the entire body, crossed the river.   Then P. Valerius commanded T. Herminius, with a small body of men, to lie concealed two miles from the city, on the Gabian road, and Sp. Lartius, with a party of light-armed troops, to post

himself at the Colline gate till the enemy should pass by,
and then to throw himself in their way so that there may be
no return to the river. The other consul, T. Lucretius,
marched out of the Nævian gate with some companies of
soldiers; Valerius himself led some chosen cohorts down
from the Cœlian mount, and they were first descried by the
enemy. Herminius, when he perceived the alarm, rose out
of the ambush and fell upon the rear of the Tuscans, who
had charged Valerius. The shout was returned on the right
and left, from the Colline gate on the one hand, and the
Nævian on the other. By this stratagem the plunderers were
put to the sword between both, they not being a match in
strength for fighting, and all the ways being blocked up to
prevent escape : this put an end to the Etrurians strolling
about in so disorderly a manner.

12. Nevertheless the blockade continued, and there was
a scarcity of corn, with a very high price. Porsena entertained a hope that by continuing the siege he should take
the city, when C. Mucius, a young nobleman, to whom it
seemed a disgrace that the Roman people, when enslaved
under kings, had never been confined within their walls in
any war nor by any enemy, should now, when a free people,
be blocked up by these very Etrurians whose armies they
had often routed, thinking that such indignity should be
avenged by some great and daring effort, at first designed,
of his own accord, to penetrate into the enemy's camp.
Then, being afraid, if he went without the permission of the
consuls, or the knowledge of any one, he might be seized
by the Roman guards and brought back as a deserter, the
circumstances of the city at the time justifying the charge,
he went to the Senate : "Fathers," says he, "I intend to
cross the Tiber, and enter the enemy's camp, if I can ; not
as a plunderer, or as an avenger in our turn of their devas-

tations. A greater deed is in my mind, if the gods assist.''
The Senate approved his design. He set out with a sword
concealed under his garment. When he came thither, he
stationed himself among the thickest of the crowd, near the
king's tribunal. There, when the soldiers were receiving
their pay, and the king's secretary sitting by him, dressed
nearly in the same style, was busily engaged, and to him
they commonly addressed themselves, being afraid to ask
which of them was Porsena, lest by not knowing the king
he should discover on himself; as fortune blindly directed
the blow, he killed the secretary instead of the king.
When, as he was going off thence where with his bloody
dagger he had made his way through the dismayed multitude, a concourse being attracted at the noise, the king's
guards immediately seized and brought him back standing
alone before the king's tribunal; even then, amidst such
menaces of fortune, more capable of inspiring dread than of
feeling it : "I am,'' says he, "a Roman citizen; my name
is Caius Mucius; an enemy, I wished to slay an enemy—nor
have I less of resolution to suffer death than I had to inflict
it. Both to act and to suffer with fortitude is a Roman's
part. Nor have I alone harbored such feelings toward you;
there is after me a long train of persons aspiring to the same
honor. Therefore, if you choose it, prepare yourself for
this peril, to contend for your life every hour; to have the
sword and the enemy in the very entrance of your pavilion;
this is the war which we, the Roman youth, declare against
you; dread not an army in array, nor a battle; the affair
will be to yourself alone and with each of us singly.''
When the king, highly incensed, and at the same time terrified at the danger, in a menacing manner commanded fires
to be kindled about him if he did not speedily explain the
plots which, by his threats, he had darkly insinuated against

6 *

him; Mucius said: "Behold me, that you may be sensible
of how little account the body is to those who have great
glory in view;" and immediately he thrusts his right hand
into the fire that was lighted for the sacrifice.   When he
continued to broil it as if he had been quite insensible, the
king, astonished at this surprising sight, after he had leaped
from his throne and commanded the young man to be removed from the altar, says: "Be gone, having acted more
like an enemy toward thyself than me.   I would encourage
thee to persevere in thy valor, if that valor stood on the
side of my country.   I now dismiss you untouched and
unhurt, exempted from the right of war."   Then Mucius,
as if making a return for the kindness, says: "Since
bravery is honored by you, so that you have obtained by
kindness that which you could not by threats, three hundred of us, the chief of the Roman youth, have conspired
to attack you in this manner.   It was my lot first.   The
rest will follow, each in his turn, according as the lot shall
set him forward, unless fortune shall afford an opportunity
of you."

13. Mucius being dismissed, to whom the cognomen of
Scævola was afterward given, from the loss of his right
hand, ambassadors from Porsena followed him to Rome.
The risk of the first attempt, from which nothing had saved
him but the mistake of the assailant, and the risk to be
encountered so often in proportion to the number of conspirators, made so strong an impression upon him, that of his
own accord he made propositions of peace to the Romans.
Mention was made to no purpose regarding the restoration
of the Tarquinii to the throne, rather because he had been
unable to refuse that to the Tarquinii than from not knowing that it would be refused to him by the Romans.   The
condition of restoring their territory to the Veientians was

obtained by him, and the necessity of giving hostages in case they wished the garrison to be withdrawn from the Janiculum was extorted from the Romans. Peace being concluded on these terms, Porsena drew his troops out of the Janiculum, and marched out of the Roman territories. The fathers gave Mucius, as a reward of his valor, lands on the other side of the Tiber, which were afterward called the Mucian meadows. By this honor paid to valor the women were excited to merit public distinctions. As the camp of the Etrurians had been pitched not far from the banks of the Tiber, a young lady named Clælia, one of the hostages, deceiving her keepers, swam over the river, amidst the darts of the enemy, at the head of a troop of virgins, and brought them all safe to their relations. When the king was informed of this, at first highly incensed, he sent deputies to Rome to demand the hostage Clælia ; that he did not regard the others ; and afterwards, being changed into admiration of her courage, he said, "that this action surpassed those of Cocles and Mucius," and declared, "as he would consider the treaty as broken if the hostage were not delivered up, so, if given up, he would send her back safe to her friends." Both sides kept their faith : the Romans restored their pledge of peace according to treaty ; and with the king of Etruria merit found not only security, but honor ; and, after making encomiums on the young lady, promised to give her, as a present, half of the hostages, and that she should choose whom she pleased. When they were all brought out, she is said to have pitched upon the young boys below puberty, which was both consonant to maiden delicacy, and, by consent of the hostages themselves, it was deemed reasonable that that age which was most exposed to injury should be freed from the enemy's hand. The peace being re-established, the Romans marked the uncommon instance of bravery in the woman by an uncommon kind of honor, an equestrian statue ; (the statue representing) a lady sitting on horseback was placed at the top of the Via Sacra.

14. Inconsistent with this so peaceful a departure of the Etrurian king from the city, is the custom handed down from the ancients, and which continues down to our times among other usages at public sales, (I mean) that of selling the goods of King Porsena ; the origin[1] of which custom must either have occurred during the war, and was not relinquished in peace, or it must have increased from a milder source than the form of expression imports, of selling the goods in a hostile manner.   Of the accounts handed down, the most probable is, that Porsena, on retiring from the Janiculum, made a present to the Romans of his camp well stored with provisions conveyed from the neighboring and fertile fields of Etruria, the city being then exhausted by the long siege ; that this, lest it should be carried away in a hostile manner, by the people being admitted in, was then sold, and called the goods of Porsena, the expression rather importing gratitude for the gift than an auction of the king's property, which never even was in the power of the Roman people.   Porsena, after ending the Roman war, that his army might not seem to have been led into these parts without effecting anything, sent his son Aruns with a part of his forces to besiege Aricia.   The matter not being expected, the Aricians were at first terrified ; afterwards assistance, which was sent for from the people of Latium and Cumæ, inspired so much hope, that they ventured to meet them in the field.   At the commencement of the battle the Etrurians attacked the Aricians so furiously, that they

[1] *The origin.* Niebuhr mentions a more probable one. See Nieb. i. p. 541 ; ii. p. 204.

routed them at the first onset. But the Cuman cohorts, opposing stratagem to force, moved off a little to one side, and when the enemy were carried beyond them in great disorder, they faced about and charged them in the rear. By this means the Etrurians, when they had almost got the victory, were inclosed and cut to pieces.[1] A very small part of them, having lost their general, because they had no nearer refuge, came to Rome without their arms, in the condition and with the air of suppliants. There they were kindly received and provided with lodgings. When their wounds were cured, many of them went home and told the kind hospitality they had met with. Affection for their hosts and for the city detained many at Rome; a place was assigned them to dwell in, which they have ever since called the Tuscan Street.

15. Then P. Lucretius and P. Valerius Publicola were elected consuls. This year ambassadors came from Porsena for the last time, regarding the restoration of Tarquin to the throne. And when they were answered that the Senate would send deputies to the king, some of the principal persons of that order were forthwith dispatched to represent to him "that it was not because the answer could not have been given in a few words that the royal family would not be received, that select members of the Senate had been deputed to him, rather than an answer given to his ambassadors at Rome; but (it was done) that all mention of the matter might be put an end to for evermore, and that their minds might not be disturbed amidst so many mutual acts of kindness, by his requiring what was adverse to the liberty

---

[1] Niebuhr thinks that from this defeat of the Etrurians may be dated the commencement of the recovery of their liberty by the Romans, and that the flight of the Roman hostages, the sale of Porsena's goods, etc., were subsequent to it.

of the Roman people, and by their denying to him to whom
they would willingly deny nothing, unless they would submit to their own ruin. That the Roman people were not
now under a kingly government, but in a state of freedom,
and were firmly determined rather to open their gates to
enemies than to kings. That it was the wish of all that
their city might have the same period of existence as their
freedom in that city. Wherefore, if he wished Rome to be
safe, they entreated that he would suffer it to be free."
The king, overcome by modesty, says: "Since it is your
firm and fixed resolve, I will neither tease you by repeatedly
urging these same subjects more frequently, nor will I disappoint the Tarquinii by holding out hopes of aid which it
is not in my power to give them ; whether they have need
of peace or of war, let them seek another place from here
for their exile, that nothing may disturb the peace between
you and me." To these kind promises he added actions
still more friendly, for he delivered up the remainder of the
hostages, and restored to them the land of the Veientians,
which had been taken from them by the treaty concluded at
Janiculum. Tarquin, all hopes of return being now cut off,
went to Tusculum to live in exile with his son-in-law, Mamilius Octavius. Thus the peace between Porsena and the
Romans was inviolably preserved.

16. M. Valerius and P. Posthumius were chosen consuls.
This year war was carried on successfully against the Sabines ; the consuls received the honor of a triumph. Upon
this the Sabines made preparations for war on a larger scale.
To make head against them, and lest any sudden danger
might arise from Tusculum (whence they suspected a war,
though it was not yet declared), P. Valerius was created
consul a fourth time, and T. Lucretius a second time. A
disturbance arising among the Sabines, between the advisers

of war and of peace, transferred from thence some additional
strength to the Romans ; for Attus Clausus afterwards called
at Rome Appius Claudius, when he himself, being an adviser of peace, was hard put to it by those who abetted the
war, and was not a match for the faction, fled from Regillum
to Rome, accompanied by a great number of clients. The
rights of citizenship and land on the other side of the Anio
were conferred on them. It was called the old Claudian
tribe, and was increased by the addition of some tribesmen
who had come from that country. Appius, being chosen
into the senate, was soon after advanced to the highest dignity of that order. The consuls having entered the territories of the Sabines with a hostile army, after they had, both
by laying waste their country, and afterwards by defeating
them in battle, so weakened the power of the enemy, that
they had no reason to dread their taking up arms again for
a long time, returned to Rome in triumph. The following
year, Agrippa Menenius and P. Posthumius being consuls,
P. Valerius, allowed by universal consent to be the ablest
man in Rome in the arts both of peace and war, died in the
height of glory, but so poor that means to defray the expenses of his funeral were wanting : he was buried at the
public charge. The matrons mourned for him as they had
done for Brutus. The same year two Latin colonies, Pometia
and Cora, revolted to the Auruncians. War was commenced
against the Auruncians, and, after defeating a numerous army
of them who boldly met the consuls entering their frontiers,
the whole Auruncian war was confined to Pometia. Nor,
after the battle was over, did they refrain from slaughter
more than in the heat of the action ; for a greater number
were slain than taken, and the prisoners they put to death
indiscriminately. Nor did the enemy, in their resentment, spare even the three hundred hostages which they

had received.   This year also the consuls triumphed at Rome.

17. The following consuls, Opiter Virginius and Sp. Cassius, first endeavored to take Pometia by storm, and afterwards by raising vineæ and other works.   But the Auruncians, prompted more by an irreconcilable hatred against them than induced by hopes of success, or by a favorable opportunity, sallied out of the town, and, though more of them were armed with lighted torches than swords, filled all places with fire and slaughter.   After they had burnt down the vineæ, slain and wounded many of the enemy, they were near killing one of the consuls, who had been thrown from his horse and severely wounded (which of them authors do not mention).   Upon this they returned to Rome, foiled in their object; the consul was left among many more who were wounded, with very uncertain hopes of his recovery.   After a short time, sufficient for curing their wounds and recruiting their army, they marched against Pometia with redoubled fury and augmented strength.   When, the vineæ having been repaired and the other apparatus of war, the soldiers were on the point of scaling the walls, the town surrendered.   Yet, though the town had surrendered, the leading men of the Auruncians, with no less cruelty than if it had been taken by assault, were beheaded indiscriminately; the others, who were colonists, were sold by auction; the town was razed, and the land sold.   The consuls obtained a triumph more from having severely gratified their revenge than in consequence of the importance of the war thus brought to a close.

18. The following year had Postumus Cominius and T. Lartius for consuls.   On this year, during the celebration of the games at Rome, as some of the courtesans were being carried off by some of the Sabine youth in a frolic, a mob

having assembled, a scuffle ensued, and almost a battle ; and
from this inconsiderable affair the whole nation seemed inclined to a renewal of hostilities.   Besides the dread of the
Latin war, this accession was further made to their fears ;
certain intelligence was received that thirty different states
had entered into a confederacy against them, at the instiga-
tion of Octavius Mamilius.   While the city was perplexed
amidst this expectation of such important events, mention
was made for the first time of nominating a dictator.   But
in what year, or who the consuls were in whom confidence
was not reposed,[1] because they were of the Tarquinian faction (for that also is recorded), or who was elected dictator
for the first time, is not satisfactorily established.   Among
the oldest writers, however, I find that Titus Lartius was
appointed the first dictator, and Spurius Cassius master of
the horse.   They chose men of consular dignity, for so the
law, made for the election of a dictator, ordained.   For this
reason, I am more inclined to believe that Lartius, who was
of consular rank, was annexed to the consuls as their direc-
tor and master, rather than Manius Valerius, the son of
Marcus and grandson of Volesus, who had not yet been
consul.   For, had they intended to choose a dictator from
that family in particular, they would much rather have
chosen his father, Marcus Valerius, a consular person, and a
man of distinguished merit.   On the creation of the dictator first at Rome, when they saw the axes carried before
him, great awe struck the common people, so that they became more submisssve to obey orders.   For neither was there
now, as under the consuls, who possessed equal power, the assistance of one of the two, nor was there appeal, nor was

---

[1] *Nec quibus consulibus parum creditum sit*, scil. fides non habita fuerit.
Arnold in his Roman History considers this to have been the true
cause of creating a dictator.

there any resource anywhere but in attentive submission. The creation of a dictator at Rome terrified the Sabines, and the more effectually, because they thought he was created on their account.[1]   Wherefore they sent ambassadors to sue for peace, to whom, when earnestly entreating the dictator and Senate to pardon the young men's offense, an answer was given that the young men could easily be forgiven, but not the old men, who continually raised one war after another. Nevertheless they continued to treat about a peace, and it would have been granted, if the Sabines would bring themselves to make good the expenses incurred on the war (for that was demanded).   War was proclaimed; a tacit truce kept the year quiet.

19. Servius Sulpicius and M. Tullius were consuls, the next year: nothing worth mentioning happened.   Then T. Æbutius and C. Vetusius.   In their consulship, Fidenæ was besieged, Crustumeria taken, and Præneste revolted from the Latins to the Romans.   Nor was the Latin war, which had been fomenting for several years, any longer deferred.   A. Postumius, dictator, and T. Æbutius his master of the horse, marching with a numerous army of horse and foot, met the enemy's forces at the Lake Regillus, in the territory of Tusculum, and, because it was heard that the Tarquins were in the army of the Latins, their rage could not be restrained, but they must immediately come to an engagement.   Accordingly the battle was more obstinate and fierce than usual; for the generals were present, not only to direct matters by their orders, but even charged one another, exposing their own persons.   And there was hardly any of the principal officers of either side who came off unwounded, except

---

[1] *Eo magis quod propter se.* From this one would be disposed to suspect that the dictator was created to take on him the management of war. See Nieb. p. 553, and Nieb. Epit. by Twiss, Append. p. 355.

the Roman dictator.   As Postumius was drawing up his men
and encouraging them in the first line, Tarquinius Superbus,
though now enfeebled by age, spurred on his horse with great
fury to attack him; but being wounded in the side, he was
carried off by a party of his own men to a place of safety.
In the other wing also, Æbutius, master of the horse, had
charged Octavius Mamilius; nor was his approach unob-
served by the Tusculan general, who also briskly spurred on
his horse to encounter him.   And such was their impetuosity, as they advanced with hostile spears, that Æbutius
was run through the arm and Mamilius struck on the breast.
The Latins received the latter into their second line ; but as
Æbutius was not able to wield his lance with his wounded
arm, he retired from the battle.   The Latin general, not in
the least discouraged by his wound, stirs up the fight; and
because he saw his own men begin to give ground, sent for
a company of Roman exiles to support them, commanded
by Tarquin's son.   This body, inasmuch as they fought
with greater fury from having been banished from their
country, and lost their estates, restored the battle for a short
time.

20. When the Romans were beginning to give ground on
that side, M. Valerius, brother to Poplicola, having observed young Tarquin boldly figuring away at the head of
his exiles, fired with the renown of his family, that the
slaying of the princes might belong to the same family
whose glory their expulsion had been, clapped spurs to his
horse, and with his javelin presented made towards Tarquin.   Tarquin retired from his violent enemy into a battalion of his own men.   As Valerius rushed rashly into
the line of the exiles, one of them ran him sideways
through the body, and as the horse was in no way retarded
by the wound of his rider, the expiring Roman fell to the

ground, his arms falling over him.   Postumius the dictator, on seeing so distinguished a man slain, the exiles advancing boldly in a body, and his own men disheartened and giving ground, gives the signal to his own cohort, a chosen body of men which he kept for the defense of his person, to treat every Roman soldier whom they should see fly from the battle as an enemy.   Upon this the Romans, by reason of the danger on both sides, turned from their flight against the enemy, and, the battle being restored, the dictator's cohort now for the first time engaged in the fight, and with fresh vigor and undaunted resolution falling on the wearied exiles, cut them to pieces.   Here another engagement took place between the leading officers.   The Latin general, on seeing the cohort of the exiles almost surrounded by the Roman dictator, advanced in haste to the front with some companies of the body of reserve. , T. Herminius, a lieutenant-general, having seen them moving in a body, and well knowing Mamilius, distinguished from the rest by his armor and dress, encountered the leader of the enemy with a force so much superior to that wherewith the general of the horse had lately done, that at one thrust he ran him through the side and slew him ; and while stripping the body of his enemy, he himself received a wound with a javelin ; and though brought back to the camp victorious, yet he died during the first dressing of it.   Then the dictator flies to the cavalry, entreating them in the most pressing terms, as the foot were tired out with fighting, to dismount from their horses and join the fight.   They obeyed his orders, dismounted, flew to the front, and, taking their post at the first line, cover themselves with their targets.   The infantry immediately recovered courage when they saw the young noblemen sustaining a share of the danger with them, the mode of fighting being now assimi-

lated.[1] Thus at length were the Latins beaten back, and
their line giving way, they retreated. The horses were
then brought up to the cavalry that they might pursue the
enemy, and the infantry likewise followed. On this the
dictator omitting nothing (that could conciliate) divine or
human aid, is said to have vowed a temple to Castor, and
likewise to have promised rewards to the first and second of
the soldiers who should enter the enemy's camp. And
such was their ardor, that the Romans took the camp with
the same impetuosity wherewith they had routed the enemy in the field. Such was the engagement at the Lake
Regillus. The dictator and master of the horse returned
to the city in triumph.

21. For the next three years there was neither settled
peace nor open war. The consuls were Q. Clælius and T.
Lartius. After them A. Sempronius and M. Minucius. In
their consulship a temple was dedicated to Saturn, and the
Saturnalia appointed to be kept as a festival. Then A.
Postumius and T. Virginius were chosen consuls. In
some authors I find that the battle at the Lake Regillus was
not fought till this year, and that A. Postumius, because
the fidelity of his colleague was suspected, laid down his
office, and thereupon was created dictator. Such great mis-
takes of dates perplex one with the history of these times,
the magistrates being arranged differently in different
writers, that you can not determine what consuls succeeded
certain consuls,[2] nor in what particular year every remarkable action happened, by reason of the antiquity, not only
of the facts, but also of the historians. Then Ap. Claudius

[1] By giving up the advantage of their horses, and forgetting their
superiority of rank.

[2] Qui consules secundum quosdam, who were the consuls that
came after certain consuls.

and P. Servilius were elected consuls. This year was remarkable for the news of Tarquin's death. He died at Cumæ, whither he had fled to the tyrant Aristodemus, after
the reduction of the power of the Latins. The Senate and
people were elated by this news. But with the Senators
their satisfaction was too extravagant, for by the chief
men among them oppression began to be practised on the
people to whom they had to that day been attentive to the
utmost of their power. The same year the colony which
King Tarquin had sent to Signia was recruited by filling up
the number of the colonists. The tribes at Rome were increased to twenty-one. And the temple of Mercury was
dedicated the fifteenth of May.

22. During the Latin war there had been neither peace
nor war with the nation of the Volscians; for both the
Volscians had raised auxiliary troops to send to the Latins,
had not so much expedition been used by the Roman dictator, and the Roman employed this expedition that he
might not have to contend in one and the same battle with
the Latin and the Volscian. In resentment of this the consuls marched their army into the Volscian territory. The
unexpected proceeding alarmed the Volscians, who dreaded
no chastisement of mere intention. Unmindful of arms,
they gave three hundred children of the principal men of
Cora and Pometia as hostages. Upon this the legions were
withdrawn, without coming to any action. Not long after
their natural disposition returned to the Volscians, now delivered of their fears. They again make secret preparation
for war, having taken the Hernicians into an alliance with
them. They send ambassadors in every direction to stir up
Latium. But the recent defeat received at the Lake Regillus could scarcely restrain the Latins from offering violence
to the ambassadors, through resentment and hatred of any

one who would advise them to take up arms. Having
seized the Volscians, they brought them to Rome. They
were there delivered up to the consuls, and information was
given that the Volscians and Hernicians were making preparations for war against the Romans. The matter being
referred to the Senate, it was so gratifying to the Senators
that they both sent back six thousand prisoners to the Latins and referred to the new magistrates the business regarding the treaty, which had been almost absolutely refused
them. Upon this, indeed, the Latins were heartily glad at
what they had done; the advisers of peace were in high esteem. They send a crown of gold to the Capitol as an offering to Jupiter. Along with the ambassadors and the offering there came a great crowd, consisting of the prisoners
who had been sent back to their friends. They proceed to
the houses of those persons with whom each had been in
servitude and return thanks for their having been generously
kept and treated during their calamity. They then form
connections of hospitality. And never at any former time
was the Latin name more closely united to the Roman state,
either by public or private ties.

23. But both the Volscian war was threatening, and the
state, being disturbed within itself, glowed with intestine
animosity between the Senate and people, chiefly on account
of those confined for debt. They complained loudly that,
while fighting abroad for liberty and dominion, they were
captured and oppressed at home by their fellow-citizens;
and that the liberty of the people was more secure in war
than in peace, among enemies than among their fellow-
citizens. And this feeling of discontent, increasing of itself,
the striking sufferings of an individual still further aggra-
vated. A certain person, advanced in years, threw himself
into the Forum with all the badges of his miseries on him.

His clothes were all over squalid, the figure of his body still more shocking, being pale and emaciated. In addition, a long beard and hair had impressed a savage wildness on his countenance ; in such wretchedness he was known notwith- standing, and they said that he had been a centurion, and, com- passionating him, they mentioned openly other distinctions (obtained) in the service ; he himself exhibited scars on his breast, testimonies of honorable battles in several places. To persons repeatedly inquiring whence that garb, whence that ghastly appearance of body (the multitude having now as- sembled around him almost like a popular assembly), he says, "that while serving in the Sabine war, because he had not only been deprived of the produce of his land in conse- quence of the depredations of the enemy, but also his resi- dence had been burned down, all his effects pillaged, his cattle driven off, a tax imposed on him at a time very dis- tressing to him, he had incurred debt ; that this debt, aggra- vated by usury, had stripped him first of his father's and grandfather's farm, then of his other property ; lastly, that a pestilence, as it were, had reached his person. That he was taken by his creditor, not into servitude, but into a house of correction and a place of execution." He then showed his back disfigured with the marks of stripes still recent. At the hearing and seeing of this a great uproar takes place. The tumult is now no longer confined to the Forum, but spreads through the entire city. Those who were confined for debt, and those who were now at their liberty, hurry into the streets from all quarters and im- plore the protection of the people. In no place is there wanting a voluntary associate of sedition. They run through all the streets in crowds to the Forum with loud shouts. Such of the Senators as happened to be in the Forum fell in with this mob with great peril to themselves ;

nor would they have refrained from violence, had not the consuls, P. Servilius and Ap. Claudius, hastily interfered to quell the disturbance. The multitude turning towards them, and showing their chains and other marks of wretchedness, said that they deserved all this, taunting them (the consuls) each with the military services performed by himself, one in one place, and another in another. They require them with menaces, rather than as suppliants, to assemble the Senate, and stand round the Senate-house in a body, determined themselves to be witnesses and directors of the public counsels. Very few of the Senators whom chance had thrown in the way were forced to attend the consuls ; fear prevented the rest from coming not only to the house but even to the Forum. Nor could anything be done by reason of the thinness of the Senate. Then, indeed, the people began to think their demand was eluded, and the redress of their grievances delayed ; that such of the Senators as had absented themselves did so not through chance or fear, but on purpose to obstruct the business. That the consuls themselves trifled with them, that their miseries were now a mere subject of mockery. By this time the sedition was come to such a height that the majesty of the consuls could hardly restrain the violence of the people. Wherefore, uncertain whether they incurred greater danger by staying at home or venturing abroad, they came at length to the Senate ; but though the house was at length full, a want of agreement manifested itself, not only among the fathers, but even between the consuls themselves. Appius, a man of violent temper, thought the matter was to be done by the authority of the consuls, and that if one or two were seized the rest would be quiet. Servilius, more inclined to moderate measures, thought that, while their minds were in this ferment, it would be both more

7

safe and more easy to bend than to break them.   Amidst these
debates another terror of a more serious nature presented
itself.

24. Some Latin horse came full speed to Rome, with the
alarming news that the Volscians were marching with a
hostile army to besiege the city, the announcement of
which (so completely had discord made the state two from
one) affected the Senators and people in a far different manner.   The people exulted with joy, and said that the gods
were come as avengers of the tyranny of the fathers.   They
encouraged one another not to enroll their names, that it
was better that all should perish together, than that they
should perish alone.   That the patricians should serve as
soldiers, that the patricians should take up arms, so that
the perils of war should remain with those with whom the
advantages were.   But the Senate, dejected and confounded
by the twofold terror, that from their own countrymen and
that from the enemy, entreated the consul Servilius, whose
temper was more conciliating, that he would extricate the
commonwealth beset with such great terrors.   Then the
consul, dismissing the Senate, proceeds into the assembly.
There he shows them that the Senate were solicitous that
care should be taken for the people's interest; but their
alarm for the whole commonwealth had interrupted their
deliberation regarding that which was no doubt the greatest
part, but yet only a part; nor could they, when the enemy
were almost at the gates, allow any thing to take precedence
of war; nor, if there should be some respite, was it either
to the credit of the people not to have taken up arms in
defense of their country unless they first receive a recom-
pense, nor consistent with the dignity of the Senators that
they adopted measures of relief for the distresses of their
countrymen through fear rather than afterwards from incli-

nation. He gave additional confidence to the assembly by
an edict, by which he ordained that no one "should detain
a Roman citizen either in chains or in prison, so as to hin-
der his enrolling his name under the consuls; and that
nobody should either seize or sell the goods of any soldier
while he was in the camp, or arrest his children or grand-
children." This ordinance being published, the debtors
under arrest who were present immediately entered their
names, and crowds of persons hastening from all quarters
of the city from their confinement, as their creditors had
no right to detain their persons, ran together into the Forum
to take the military oath. These made up a considerable
body of men ; nor was the bravery or activity of the others
more conspicuous in the Volscian war. The consul led out
his army against the enemy, and pitched his camp at a little
distance from them.

25. The next night the Volscians, relying on the dissension among the Romans, made an attempt on their camp,
to see if any desertion or treachery might be resorted to
during the night. The sentinels on guard perceived them ;
the army was called up, and the signal being given they ran
to arms. Thus that attempt of the Volscians was frustrated ; the remainder of the night was dedicated to repose on
both sides. The next morning at daybreak the Volscians,
having filled the trenches, attacked the rampart. And
already the fortifications were being demolished on every
side, when the consul, although all on every side, and more
especially the debtors, cried out that he should give the
signal, having delayed a little while for the purpose of try- .
ing the feelings of the soldiers, when their great ardor became sufficiently apparent, having at length given the signal
for sallying forth, he lets out the soldiers, now impatient
for the fight. At the very first onset the enemy were routed ;

the rear of them, who fled, was harassed, as long as the infantry was able to overtake them ; the cavalry drove them
in consternation to their very camp.   In a little time the
camp itself was taken and plundered, the legions having
surrounded it, as the panic had driven the Volscians even
from thence also.   On the next day the legions being led
to Suessa Pometia, whither the enemy had retreated, in a
few days the town is taken ; when taken, it was given up
for plunder ; by these means the needy soldiers were somewhat relieved.   The consul leads back his victorious army
to Rome with the greatest glory to himself : as he is setting
out for Rome, the deputies of the Ecetrans (a part) of the
Volscians, alarmed for their state after the taking of Pometia, come to him.   By a decree of the Senate peace is
granted them, but their land is taken from them.

26.   Immediately after the Sabines also caused an alarm
to the Romans ; but it was rather a tumult than a war.   It
was announced in the city during the night that a Sabine
army had advanced as far as the River Anio, plundering the
country ; that the country houses there were pillaged and
burned down indiscriminately.   A. Postumius, who had
been dictator in the Latin war, was immediately sent against
them with all the horse.   The consul Servilius followed him
with a chosen body of foot.   The cavalry cut off most of the
stragglers ; nor did the Sabine legion make any resistance
against the foot when they came up with them.   Being tired,
both by their march and their plundering the country in
the night, and a great number of them being surfeited with
eating and drinking in the cottages, they had scarcely sufficient strength for flight.   The Sabine war being thus heard
of and finished in one night, on the following day, amidst
sanguine hope of peace being secured in every quarter, ambassadors from the Auruncians come to the Senate, pro-

claiming war unless the troops are withdrawn from the Volscian territory. The army of the Auruncians had set out
from home simultaneously with the ambassadors ; the report
of which having been seen not far from Aricia, excited such
a tumult among the Romans, that neither the Senate could
be consulted in regular form, nor could they, while themselves taking up arms, give a pacific answer to those advancing against them in arms. They march to Aricia with a
determined army, come to an engagement not far from
thence, and in one battle put an end to the war.

27. After the defeat of the Auruncians, the people of
Rome, victorious in so many wars within a few days, were
expecting the promises of the consul and the engagement
of the Senate (to be made good). But Appius, both through
his natural pride, and in order to undermine the credit of
his colleague, issued his decrees regarding borrowed money
with all possible severity. And from this time both those
who had been formerly in confinement were delivered up to
their creditors, and others also were taken into custody.
When this happened to a soldier, he appealed to the colleague, and a crowd gathered about Servilius : they represented to him his promises, severally upbraided him with
their services in war, and with the scars they had received.
They loudly called upon him to lay the matter before the
Senate, and that, as consul, he would relieve his fellow-
citizens; as a general, his soldiers. These remonstrances
affected the consul, but the situation of affairs obliged him
to back out; so completely had not only his colleague, but
the whole body of the patricians, adopted an entirely opposite course. And thus, by acting a middle part, he neither
escaped the odium of the people nor gained the favor of the
Senators. The fathers looked upon him as a weak, popu-
larity-hunting consul, and the people considered him as a

deceiver. And it soon appeared that he was as odious to them as Appius himself. A dispute had happened between the consuls as to which should dedicate the Temple of Mercury. The Senate referred the affair from themselves to the people, and ordained that to whichsoever of them the dedication should be granted by order of the people, he should preside over the markets, establish a company of merchants, and perform the functions of a pontifex maximus. The people gave the dedication of the temple to M. Lætorius, the centurion of the first legion, that it might plainly appear to have been done not so much out of respect to a person on whom an honor above his rank had been conferred as to affront the consuls. Upon this one of the consuls particularly, and the Senators, were highly incensed. But the people had acquired courage, and proceeded in a manner quite different from what they had at first intended. For when they despaired of redress from the consuls and Senate, upon seeing a debtor led to the court, they flew together from all quarters. And neither the decree of the consul could be heard in consequence of the noise and clamor, nor, when he had pronounced the decree, did any one obey it. All was managed by violence, and the entire dread and danger with respect to personal liberty was transferred from the debtors to the creditors, who were severally abused by the crowd in the very sight of the consul. In addition to all this, the dread of the Sabine war spread, and, when a levy was decreed, nobody gave in his name; Appius being enraged, and bitterly inveighing against the ambitious arts of his colleague, who by his popular silence was betraying the republic, and besides his not passing sentence against the debtors, likewise neglected to raise the levies, after they had been voted by the Senate. Yet he declared that "the commonwealth was not entirely deserted, nor the

consular authority altogether debased.   That he alone
would vindicate both his own dignity and that of the Senators." When a daily mob, emboldened by licentiousness,
stood round him, he commanded a noted ringleader of the
sedition to be apprehended.   He, as the lictors were carrying him off, appealed to the people; nor would the consul
have allowed the appeal, because there was no doubt regarding the judgment of the people, had not his obstinacy been
with difficulty overcome, rather by the advice and influence
of the leading men than by the clamors of the people; so
much resolution he had to bear the weight of their odium.
The evil gained ground daily, not only by open clamors,
but, which was far more dangerous, by a secession and by
secret meetings.   At length the consuls, so odious to the
commons, went out of office: Servilius liked by neither party,
Appius highly esteemed by the Senators.

28. Then A. Virginius and T. Vetusius enter on the consulship.   Upon this the commons, uncertain what sort of
consuls they were to have, held nightly meetings, some of
them upon the Esquiline, and others upon the Aventine
hill, that they might not be confused by hasty resolutions
in the Forum, or take their measures inconsiderately and
without concert.   The consuls, judging this proceeding to
be of dangerous tendency, as it really was, laid the matter
before the Senate.   But they were not allowed, after pro-
posing it, to take the votes regularly; so tumultuously was
it received on all sides by the clamors and indignation of
the fathers, at the consuls throwing on the Senate the odium
of that which should have been put down by consular
authority.   "That if there really were magistrates in the
republic, there would have been no council in Rome but the
public one.   That the republic was now divided and split
into a thousand Senate-houses and assemblies, some of which

were held on the Esquiline, others on the Aventine hill.
That one man—in truth such as Appius Claudius, for that
that was more than a consul—would in a moment disperse
these private meetings." When the consuls, thus rebuked,
asked them, "What they desired them to do, for that they
would act with as much energy and vigor as the Senators
wished," they resolve that they should push on the levies
as briskly as possible, that the people were become insolent
from want of employment. When the house broke up, the
consuls ascend the tribunal and summon the young men by
name. But none of them made any answer, and the people
crowding round them, as if in a general assembly, said,
"That the people would no longer be imposed on. They
should never list one soldier till the public faith was made
good. That liberty should be restored to each before arms
were given, that they might fight for their country and fellow-citizens, and not for arbitrary lords." The consuls
fully understood the orders they had received from the
Senate, but they saw none of those who had talked so big
within the walls of the Senate-house present themselves to
take any share with them in the public odium. A desperate
contest with the commons seemed at hand. Therefore, before they would have recourse to extremities, they thought it
advisable to consult the Senate a second time. Then, indeed, the younger Senators flocked in a hurry round the
chairs of the consuls, commanding them to abdicate the
consulate, and resign an office which they had not courage
to support.

29. Having sufficiently tried both ways,[1] the consuls at
length said: "Conscript fathers, lest you may say that you
were not forewarned, a great disturbance is at hand. We
require that they who accuse us most severely of cowardice

[1] The determination of the plebeians and Senators.

would assist us in raising the levies; we shall proceed according to the resolution of the most intrepid among you, since it so pleases you." They return to their tribunal, and on purpose commanded one of the most factious of the people, who stood in their view, to be called upon by name. When he stood mute, and a number of men stood round him in a ring, to prevent his being seized, the consuls sent a lictor to him. He being repulsed, such of the fathers as attended the consuls, exclaiming against it as an intolerable insult, ran in a hurry from the tribunal to assist the lictor. But when the violence was turned from the lictor, who suffered nothing else but being prevented from seizing him, against the fathers, the riot was quelled by the interposition of the consuls, in which, however, without stones or weapons, there was more noise and angry words than mischief done. The Senate, called in a tumultuous manner, is consulted in a manner still more tumultuous; such as had been beaten, calling out for an inquiry, and the most violent members declaring their sentiments no less by clamors and noise than by their votes. At length, when their passion had subsided, the consuls reproaching them with there being as much disorderly conduct in the Senate as in the Forum, the house began to vote in regular order. There were three different opinions: P. Virginius did not make the matter general.[1] He voted that they should consider only those who, relying on the promise of P. Servilius the consul, had served in a war against the Auruncians and Sabines. Titius Largius was of opinion, "That it was not now a proper time to reward services only. That all the people were immersed in debt, and that a stop could not be put to the evil unless measures were adopted for all. And that if the condition of different parties be different, the divisions would

[1] *Rem non vulgabat*, was not for extending the relief to all.

7 *

rather be thereby inflamed than composed." Appius
Claudius, who was naturally severe, and, by the hatred of
the commons on the one hand, and praises of the Senators
on the other, was become quite infuriated, said, "That
these riots proceeded not from distress, but from licentiousness; that the people were rather wanton than violent; that
this terrible mischief took its rise from the right of appeal;
since threats, not authority, was all that belonged to the
consuls, while permission was given to appeal to those who
were accomplices in the crime.   Come," added he, "let us
create a dictator from whom there lies no appeal; this mad-
ness, which hath set every thing in a flame, will immediately
subside.   Let any one dare, then, to strike a lictor, when he
shall know that his back, and even his life, are in the power
of that person whose authority he has insulted."

30. To many the opinion of Appius appeared, as it really
was, severe and violent.   On the other hand, those of Virginius and Largius were not safe for the precedent they established; especially they thought that of Largius so, as it
would destroy all credit.   The opinion of Virginius was
reckoned to be most moderate, and a happy medium between
the other two.   But through the spirit of faction and a
regard of private interest, which always have and always
will obstruct the public councils, Appius prevailed, and was
himself near being created dictator; which step would certainly have alienated the commons at this most dangerous
juncture, when the Volsci, the Æqui, and the Sabines happened to be all in arms at the same time.   But the consuls
and elder Senators took care that this office, in its own nature uncontrollable, should be committed to a man of moderate temper.   They choose Manius Valerius, son of Volesus,
dictator.   The people, though they saw that this magistrate
was created against themselves, yet, as they had got the right

of appeal by his brother's law, dreaded nothing oppressive or
tyrannical from that family.   An edict of the dictator's
which was almost the same with that published by the consul Servilius, afterwards confirmed their minds.   But judging it safer to confide in both the man and in the absolute
power with which he was vested, they gave in their names,
desisting from all contest.   Ten legions were levied, a greater
army than had ever been raised before.   Each of the consuls
had three legions assigned him, and the dictator commanded
four.   Nor could the war be deferred any longer.   The Æqui
had made incursions upon the Latin territory ; the deputies
of the Latins begged the Senate either to send them assistance, or to allow them to arm themselves for the purpose of
defending their own frontiers.   It seemed safer that the
Latins should be defended without arming than to allow
them to take up arms again.   Wherefore Vetusius the consul was sent to their assistance ; this immediately put a stop
to the devastations.   The Æqui retired from the plains, and,
depending more on the advantage of the ground than on
their arms, secured themselves on the summits of the mountains.   The other consul, having marched against the Volsci,
in order that he too might not waste time, challenged the
enemy to pitch their camp nigh to his, and to risk an engagement by ravaging their lands.   Both armies stood in
order of battle before their lines in a plain between the two
camps.   The Volsci had considerably the advantage in
number.   Accordingly, they rushed on to the fight in a
careless manner, and as if contemptuously.   The Roman
consul neither advanced his forces, and, not suffering the
enemy's shouts to be returned, he ordered them to stand
still with their spears fixed in the ground, and, when the
enemy came up, to draw their swords and fall upon them
with all their force.   The Volsci, wearied with running

and shouting, set upon the Romans as if they had been quite benumbed through fear; but when they found the vigorous resistance that was made, and saw their swords glittering before their face, they turned their backs in great disorder, just as if they had fallen into an ambuscade.   Nor had they strength sufficient even for flight, as they had advanced to the battle in full speed.   The Romans, on the other hand, as they had not stirred from their ground in the beginning of the action, being fresh and vigorous, easily overtook the enemy, who were weary, took their camp by assault, and, after driving them thence, pursued them to Velitræ, into which the conquered and conquerors entered in a body.   By the promiscuous slaughter which was here made of all ranks, there was more blood spilt than in the battle itself.   Quarter was given to a small number of them, who threw down their arms and surrendered.

31. While these things are going on among the Volsci, the dictator routs, puts to flight, and strips of their camp, the Sabines, where by far the most serious part of the war lay.   By a charge of his cavalry he had thrown into confusion the centre of the enemy's line, where, by the wings extending themselves too far, they had not strengthened their line by a suitable depth of files.[1]   The infantry fell upon them in this confusion; by one and the same charge their camp was taken and the war concluded.   There was no other battle in those times more memorable than this since the action at the Lake Regillus.   The dictator is borne into the city in triumph.   Besides the usual honors, a place in the circus was assigned to him and his descendants to see the public games; a curule chair was fixed in that place.   The lands of Velitræ were taken from the conquered Volsci; colonists were sent from the city to Velitræ, and a colony

[1] *I.e.*, by deepening the files.

planted there.   Soon after there was an engagement with the
Æqui, but contrary to the wish of the consul, because they
had to approach the enemy by disadvantageous ground.
But the soldiers complaining that the war was on purpose
spun out, that the dictator might resign his office before
they returned home to the city, and so his promises might
fall to the ground without effect, as those of the consul had
done before, forced him at all hazards to march his army up
the hill.   This imprudent step, by the cowardice of the
enemy, turned out successfully ; for before the Romans
came within reach of a dart, the Æqui, quite amazed at
their boldness, abandoned their camp, which was situated
in a very strong position, and ran down into the valleys on
the opposite side.[1]   In it abundance of booty was found, and
the victory was a bloodless one.   Matters being thus successfully managed in war in three different directions, anxiety
respecting the event of their domestic differences had left
neither the Senators nor the people.   With such powerful
influence, and with such art also, had the money-lenders
made their arrangements, so as to disappoint not only the
people, but even the dictator himself.   For Valerius, after the
return of the consul Vetusius, first of all matters brought before the Senate that relating to the victorious people, and
proposed the question, what it was their determination
should be done with respect to those confined for debt.   And
when this motion was rejected, "I am not acceptable," says
he, "as an adviser of concord.   You will ere long wish, depend on it, that the commons of Rome had patrons similar
to me.   For my part, I will neither further disappoint my
fellow-citizens nor will I be dictator to no purpose.   Intes-

---

[1] "On the opposite side."   Gronovius proposes, instead of ad-
versus, to read aversas: scil. the valleys behind them, or in their
rear.

tine dissensions, foreign wars, caused the republic to require such a magistrate. Peace has been secured abroad, it is impeded at home. I will be a witness to disturbance as a private citizen, rather than as dictator." Then quitting the Senate-house, he abdicated his dictatorship. The case appeared to the commons that he had resigned his office indignant at the treatment shown to them. Accordingly, as if his engagements to them had been fully discharged, since it had not been his fault that they were not made good, they attended him when returning to his home with approbation and applause.

32. Fear then seized the Senators lest, if the army should be dismissed, secret meetings and conspiracies would be renewed; wherefore, though the levy had been held by the dictator, yet supposing that, as they had sworn obedience to the consuls, the soldiers were bound by their oath, under the pretext of hostilities being renewed by the Æqui, they ordered the legions to be led out of the city; by which proceeding the sedition was hastened. And it is said that at first it was in contemplation to put the consuls to death, that they might be discharged from their oath; but that being afterward informed that no religious obligation could be dissolved by a criminal act, they, by the advice of one Sicinius, retired, without the orders of the consuls, to the sacred mount beyond the River Anio, three miles from the city: this account is more general than that which Piso has given, that the secession was made to the Aventine. There, without any leader, their camp being fortified with a rampart and trench, remaining quiet, taking nothing but what was necessary for sustenance, they kept themselves for several days, neither being attacked nor attacking others. Great was the panic in the city, and through mutual fear all was suspense. The people left in the city dreaded the vio-

lence of the Senators ; the Senators dreaded the people remaining in the city, uncertain whether they should prefer
them to stay or to depart ; but how long would the multitude which had seceded remain quiet ? what were to be the
consequences then, if, in the mean time, any foreign war
should break out ? they certainly considered no hope left,
save in the concord of the citizens ; this should be restored
to the state by fair or by unfair means. It was resolved,
therefore, that there should be sent as ambassador to the
people Menenius Agrippa, an eloquent man, and one who
was a favorite with the people, because he derived his origin
from them. He, being admitted into the camp, is said to
have related to them merely the following story in that anti-
quated and uncouth style : "At a time when all the parts in
the human body did not, as now, agree together, but the
several members had each its own scheme, its own language,
the other parts, indignant that every thing was procured for
the belly by their care, labor, and service ; that the belly,
remaining quiet in the centre, did nothing but enjoy the
pleasures afforded it. They conspired accordingly, that the
hands should not convey food to the mouth, nor the mouth
receive it when presented, nor the teeth chew it : while they
wished, under the influence of this feeling, to subdue the
belly by famine, the members themselves and the entire
body were reduced to the last degree of emaciation. Thence
it became apparent that the service of the belly was by no
means a slothful one; that it did not so much receive nourishment as supply it, sending to all parts of the body this blood
by which we live and possess vigor, distributed equally to
the veins when perfected by the digestion of the food." By
comparing in this way how similar the intestine sedition of
the body was to the resentment of the people against the Senators, he made an impression on the minds of the multitude.

33. Then a commencement was made to treat of a reconciliation, and among the conditions it was allowed "that
the commons should have their own magistrates, with inviolable privileges, who should have the power of bringing
assistance against the consuls, and that it should not be lawful for any of the patricians to hold that office." Thus two
tribunes of the commons were created, Caius Licinius and
L. Albinus. These created three colleagues for themselves.
It is clear that among these was Sicinius, the adviser of the
sedition ; with respect to two, who they were is not so clear.
There are some who say that only two tribunes were elected
on the sacred mount, and that there the devoting law was
passed. During the secession of the commons, Sp. Cassius
and Postumus Cominius entered on the consulship. During
their consulate the treaty with the Latin states was concluded. To ratify this, one of the consuls remained at
Rome ; the other, being sent to the Volscian war, routs and
puts to flight the Volscians of Antium ; and continuing his
pursuit of them, now that they were driven into the town of
Longula, he takes possession of the town. Next he took
Polusca, also belonging to the Volscians ; then he attacked
Corioli, with all his force. There was then in the camp,
among the young noblemen, C. Marcius, a youth distinguished both for intelligence and courage, who afterwards
attained the cognomen of Coriolanus. When, as the Roman
army was besieging Corioli, and was wholly intent on the
townspeople, whom they kept shut up, without any apprehension of war threatening from without, the Volscian
legion, setting out from Antium, suddenly attacked them,
and, at the same time the enemy sallied forth from the town,
Marcius happened to be on guard. He, with a chosen body
of men, not only repelled the attack of those who had sallied out, but boldly rushed in through the open gate, and

having cut down all in the part of the city nearest him, and
having hastily seized some fire, threw it in the houses adjoining to the wall.   Upon this the shouts of the townsmen
mingling with the wailings of the women and children, occasioned by the first fright,[1] as is usual, both increased the
courage of the Romans and dispirited the Volscians, seeing
the city captured to the relief of which they had come.
Thus the Volsci of Antium were defeated, the town of Corioli was taken.   And so much did Marcius, by his valor,
eclipse the reputation of the consul, that, had not the treaty
concluded with the Latins by Sp. Cassius alone, because his
colleague was absent, served as a memorial of it, it would
have been forgotten that Postumus Cominius had conducted
the war with the Volscians.   The same year dies Agrippa
Menenius, a man during all his life equally a favorite with
the Senators and commons, still more endeared to the commons after the secession.   To this man, the mediator and
umpire in restoring concord among his countrymen, the
ambassador of the Senators to the commons, the person who
brought back the commons to the city, were wanting the expenses of his funeral.   The people buried him by the con-
tribution of a sextans from each person.

34. T. Geganius and P. Minutius were next elected consuls.   In this year, when everything was quiet from war
abroad, and the dissensions were healed at home, another
much more serious evil fell upon the state ; first a scarcity
of provisions, in consequence of the lands lying untilled
during the secession of the commons ; then a famine such as
befalls those who are besieged.   And it would have ended in
the destruction of the slaves at least, and indeed some of the
commons also, had not the consuls adopted precautionary

---

[1] I have here adopted the reading of Stocker and others, scil. *ad
terrorem, ut solet, primum ortus.*

measures by sending persons in every direction to buy up
corn, not only into Etruria, on the coast to the right of
Ostia, and through the Volscians, along the coast on.the left
as far as Cumæ, but into Sicily also, in quest of it. So far
had the hatred of their neighbors obliged them to stand in
need of aid from distant countries.   When corn had been
bought up at Cumæ, the ships were detained in lieu of the
property of the Tarquinii by the tyrant Aristodemus, who
was their heir. Among the Volsci and in the Pomptine
territory it could not even be purchased.   The corn dealers
themselves incurred danger from the violence of the inhabitants.   Corn came from Etruria by the Tiber ; by means of
this the people were supported. Amidst this distressing
scarcity they would have been harassed by a very inconve-
nient war, had not a dreadful pestilence attacked the Volsci
when about to commence hostilities.   The minds of the
enemy being alarmed by this calamity, so that they were influenced by some terror, even after it had abated, the Romans
both augmented the number of their colonists at Velitræ,
and dispatched a new colony to the mountains of Norba, to
serve as a barrier in the Pomptine district.   Then, in the
consulship of M. Minucius and A. Sempronius, a great quantity of corn was imported from Sicily, and it was debated in
the Senate at what rate it should be given to the commons.
Many were of opinion that the time was come for putting
down the commons, and for recovering those rights which
had been wrested from the Senators by secession and violence.   In particular, Marcius Coriolanus, an enemy to
tribunitian power, says : " If they desire the former rate of
provisions, let them restore to the Senators their former
rights.   Why do I, after being sent under the yoke, after being, as it were, ransomed from robbers, behold plebeian magistrates, and Sicinius invested with power ? Shall I submit

to these indignities longer than is necessary? Shall I, who
would not have endured King Tarquin, tolerate Sicinius?
Let him now secede ; let him call away the commons. The
road lies open to the sacred mount and to other hills. Let
them carry off the corn from our lands, as they did three
years since. Let them have the benefit of that scarcity
which in their frenzy they have occasioned. I will venture
to say that, brought to their senses by these sufferings, they
will themselves become tillers of the lands, rather than,
taking up arms and seceding, they would prevent them from
being tilled." It is not so easy to say whether it should
have been done, as I think that it might have been practi-
cable for the Senators, on the condition of lowering the price
of provisions, to have rid themselves of both the tribunitian
power, and all the restraints imposed on them against their
will.[1]

35. This proposal both appeared to the Senate too harsh,
and from exasperation well nigh drove the people to arms :
"That they were now assailed with famine, as if enemies ;
that they were defrauded of food and sustenance ; that the
foreign corn, the only support which fortune unexpectedly
furnished to them, was being snatched from their mouth,
unless the tribunes were given up in chains to C. Marcius,
unless he glut his rage on the backs of the commons of
Rome. That in him a new executioner had started up, who
ordered them to die or be slaves." An assault would have
been made on him as he left the Senate-house, had not the
tribunes very opportunely appointed him a day for trial ;

[1] *l.c.*, I think it might have been done ; whether it would have
been right to do so, it is not so easy to decide. Livy means to say that
it was possible enough for the Senators, by lowering the price of
corn, to get rid of the tribunes, etc. Such a judgment is easily
formed ; it is not, however, he says, so easy to determine whether it
would have been expedient to follow the advice of Coriolanus.

by this their rage was suppressed, every one saw himself become the judge, the arbiter of the life and death of his foe. At first Marcius heard the threats of the tribunes with contempt. "That the right to afford aid, not to inflict punishment, had been granted to that office; that they were tribunes of the commons, and not of the Senators." But the commons had risen with such violent determination, that the Senators were obliged to extricate themselves from danger by the punishment of one.[1] They resisted, however, in spite of popular odium, and employed each individual his own powers, and all those of the entire order. And, first, the trial was made whether they could upset the affair by posting their clients (in several places), by deterring individuals from attending meetings and cabals.   Then they all proceeded in a body (you would suppose that all the Senators were on their trial), earnestly entreating the commons that, if they would not acquit as innocent, they would at least pardon as guilty, one citizen, one Senator. As he did not attend on the day appointed, they persevered in their resentment. Being condemned in his absence, he went into exile to the Volsci, threatening his country, and even then breathing all the resentment of an enemy. The Volsci received him kindly on his arrival, and treated him still more kindly every day in proportion as his resentful feelings towards his countrymen became more striking, and one time frequent complaints, another time threats were heard. He lodged with Attius Tullus. He was then the chief man of the Volscian people, and always a determined enemy of the Romans. Thus, when old animosity stimulated the one, recent resentment the other, they concert schemes for (bring-

---

[1] *I.e.*, the Senate found themselves reduced to the necessity of delivering one up to the vengeance of the people, in order to save themselves from the further consequences of plebeian rage.

ing about) a war with Rome. They did not at once believe that their people could be persuaded to take up arms, so often unsuccessfully tried. That by the many frequent wars, and lastly, by the loss of their youth in the pestilence, their spirits were now broken ; that they must have recourse to art, in a case where animosity had become blunted from length of time, that their feelings might become exasperated by some fresh cause of resentment.

36. It happened that preparations were being made at Rome for a repetition of the great games.[1]   The cause of repeating them was this : on the morning of the games, the show not yet being commenced, a master of a family, after flogging his slave loaded with a neck-yoke, had driven him through the middle of the circus ; after this the games were commenced, as if that circumstance bore no relation to religion. Not long after Tit. Atinius, a plebeian, had a dream. Jupiter seemed to him to say : "That the person who danced previous to the games had displeased him ; unless these games were renewed on a splendid scale, that the city would be in danger ; that he should go and announce these things to the consuls." Though his mind was not altogether free from superstitious feelings, his respectful awe of the dignity of the magistrates overcame his religious fear, lest he might pass into the mouths of people as a laughing-stock. This delay cost him dear ; for he lost his son within a few days ; and, lest the cause of this sudden calamity should be doubtful, that same phantom, presenting itself to him sorrowful in mind, seemed to ask him, whether he had received a sufficient requital for his contempt of the deity ; that a still heavier one awaited him, unless he went immediately and delivered the message to the consuls. The matter was now still more pressing. Hesitating, however,

[1] The same as the Circenses.

and delaying, he was at length overtaken by a severe stroke
of disease—a sudden paralysis. Then, indeed, the anger of
the gods aroused him. Wearied out, therefore, by his past
sufferings and by those threatening him, having convened a
meeting of his friends, after he had detailed to them all he
had seen and heard, and Jupiter's having so often presented
himself to him in his sleep, the threats and anger of Heaven
realized[1] in his own calamities, by the unhesitating assent of
all who were present he. is conveyed in a litter into the
Forum to the consuls; from thence being conveyed into
the Senate-house, after he had stated those same particu-
lars to the Senators, to the great surprise of all, behold
another miracle : he who had been conveyed into the Senate-
house deprived of the use of all his limbs, is recorded to
have returned home on his own feet after he discharged his
duty.

37. The Senate decreed that the games should be celebrated on as grand a scale as possible. To these games a
great number of Volscians came by the advice of Attius
Tullus. Before the games were commenced, Tullus, as had
been concerted at home with Marcius, comes to the consuls.
He tells them that there were matters on which he wished
to treat with them in private concerning the commonwealth.
All witnesses being removed, he says : "With reluctance I
say that of my countrymen which is rather disparaging.[2] I
do not, however, come to allege against them any thing as
having been committed by them, but to guard against their
committing any thing. The minds of our people are far
more fickle than I could wish. We have felt that by many .
disasters ; seeing that we are still preserved, not through

[1] *Realized—repræsentatas*—quasi præsentes factas, oculis subjectas—
presented as it were to the sight.—*Rasch.*

[2] *Sequius sit*—otherwise than as it should be.

our own deserts, but through your forbearance. There is now here a great multitude of Volscians. The games are going on ; the city will be intent on the exhibition. I remember what has been committed in this city on a similar occasion by the youth of the Sabines. My mind shudders lest any thing should be committed inconsiderately and rashly. I considered that these matters should be mentioned beforehand to you, consuls. With regard to myself, it is my determination to depart hence home immediately, lest, if present, I may be affected by the contagion of any word or deed." Having said this, he departed. When the consuls laid before the Senate the matter, doubtful with respect to proof, though from credible authority, the authority more than the thing itself, as usually happens, urged them to adopt even needless precautions ; and a decree of the Senate being passed that the Volscians should quit the city, criers are sent in different directions to order them all to depart before night. A great panic struck them, at first, as they ran about to their lodgings to carry away their effects. Afterwards, when setting out, indignation arose in their breasts : "That they, as if polluted with crime and contaminated, were driven away from the games on festival days, from the converse in a manner of men and gods."

38. As they went along in an almost continuous body, Tullus having preceded them to the fountain of Ferentina, accosting the chiefs among them according as each arrived, by asking questions and expressing indignation, he led both themselves, who greedily listened to language congenial to their angry feelings,[1] and through them the rest of the multitude, into a plain adjoining to the road. There having

[1] *Audientes secunda iræ verba*—attentively listening to words which fanned (or chimed in with) their anger.—*St.*

commenced an address after the manner of a public harangue, he says: "Though you were to forget the former ill
treatment of the Roman people and the calamities of the
nation of the Volsci, and all other such matters, with what
feelings do you bear this outrage offered you to-day, whereon
they have commenced their games by insulting us? Have
you not felt that a triumph has been had over you this day?
that you, when departing, were a spectacle to all—citizens,
foreigners, so many neighboring states? that your wives,
your children, were exhibited before the eyes of men? What
do you suppose to have been the sentiments of those who
heard the voice of the crier? what of those who saw you
departing? what of those who met this ignominious caval-
cade? what, except that we are identified with some enor-
mous guilt by which we should profane the games, and
render an expiation necessary; that for this reason we are
driven away from the residences of these pious people, from
their converse and meeting? what, does it not strike you
that we still live because we hastened our departure? if this
is a departure, and not a flight. And do you not consider
this to be the city of enemies, where, if you had delayed a
single day, you must have all died? War has been declared
against you; to the heavy injury of those who declared it,
if you are men." Thus, being both already charged with
resentment and incited (by this harangue), they went severally to their homes, and, by instigating each his own
state, they succeeded in making the entire Volscian nation
revolt.

39. The generals selected for that war by the unanimous
choice of all the states were Attius Tullus and Caius Marcius; in the latter of whom their chief hope was reposed.
And this hope he by no means disappointed: so that it
clearly appeared that the Roman commonwealth was more

powerful by reason of its generals than its army. Having marched to Circeii, he expelled from thence the Roman colonists, and delivered that city in a state of freedom to the Volscians. From thence passing across the country through by-roads into the Latin way, he deprived the Romans of their recently-acquired towns—Satricum, Longula, Polusca, Corioli. He next retook Lavinium : he then took in succession Corbio, Vitellia, Trebia, Lavici, and Pedum. Lastly he marches from Pedum to the city,[1] and having pitched his camp at the Cluilian trenches, five miles from the city, he from thence ravages the Roman territory, guards being sent among the devastators to preserve the lands of the patricians intact ; whether as being incensed chiefly against the plebeians, or in order that dissension might arise between the Senators and the people. And this certainly would have arisen, so powerfully did the tribunes, by inveighing against the leading men of the state, incite the plebeians, already sufficiently violent of themselves ; but their apprehensions of the foe, the strongest bond of concord, united their minds, distrustful and rancorous though they were. The only matter not agreed on was this, that the Senate and consuls rested their hopes on nothing else than on arms ; the plebeians preferred any thing to war. Sp. Nautius and Sex. Furius were now consuls. While they were reviewing the legions, posting guards along the walls and other places where they had determined that there should be posts and watches, a vast

---

[1] Scil. Rome. Dionysius narrates the expedition of Coriolanus in a different order from that given by Livy, and says that he approached the city twice. Niebuhr, ii. p. 94, n. 535, thinks that the words " passing across the country into the Latin way " (in Latinam viam transversis itineribus transgressus) have been transposed from their proper place, and that they should come in after "he then took," etc. (tunc deinceps).

8

multitude of persons demanding peace terrified them, first, by their seditious clamor ; then compelled them to convene the Senate, to consider the question of sending ambassadors to C. Marcius. The Senate entertained the question, when it became evident that the spirits of the plebeians were giving way, and, ambassadors being sent to Marcius concerning peace, brought back a harsh answer: "If their lands were restored to the Volscians, that they might then consider the question of peace ; if they were disposed to enjoy the plunder of war at their ease, that he, mindful both of the injurious treatment of his countrymen, as well as of the kindness of strangers, would do his utmost to make it appear that his spirit was irritated by exile, not crushed." When the same persons are sent back a second time, they are not admitted into the camp. It is recorded that the priests also, arrayed in their insignia, went as suppliants to the enemy's camp, and that they did not influence his mind more than the ambassadors.

40. Then the matrons assemble in a body around Veturia, the mother of Coriolanus, and his wife, Volumnia : whether that was the result of public counsel or of the women's fear, I can not ascertain.   They certainly carried their point that Veturia, a lady advanced in years, and Volumnia, leading her two sons by Marcius, should go into the camp of the enemy, and that women should defend by entreaties and tears a city which men were unable to defend by arms. When they reached the camp, and it was announced to Coriolanus that a great body of women were approaching, he, who had been moved neither by the majesty of the state in its ambassadors nor by the sanctity of religion so strikingly addressed to his eyes and understanding in its priests, was much more obdurate against the women's tears.   Then one of his acquaintances, who recognized Veturia, distinguished

from all the others by her sadness, standing between her
daughter-in-law and grand-children, says: "Unless my eyes
deceive me, your mother, children, and wife are approaching." When Coriolanus, almost like one bewildered, rushing in consternation from his seat, offered to embrace his
mother as she met him, the lady, turning from entreaties to
angry rebuke, says: "Before I receive your embrace, let
me know whether I have come to an enemy or to a son;
whether I am in your camp a captive or a mother? Has
length of life and a hapless old age reserved me for this—
to behold you an exile, then an enemy? Could you lay
waste this land, which gave you birth and nurtured you?
Though you had come with an incensed and vengeful mind,
did not your resentment subside when you entered its frontiers? When Rome came within view, did it not occur to
you, within these walls my house and guardian gods are,
my mother, wife and children? So then, had I not been a
mother, Rome would not be besieged; had I not a son, I
might have died free in a free country. But I can now suffer
nothing that is not more discreditable to you than distressing to me; nor, however wretched I may be, shall I be so
long. Look to these, whom, if you persist, either an untimely death or lengthened slavery awaits." Then his wife
and children embraced him; and the lamentation proceeding from the entire crowd of women, and their bemoaning
themselves and their country, at length overcame the man;
then, after embracing his family, he sends them away; he
moved his camp farther back from the city. Then, after
he had drawn off his troops from the Roman territory,
they say that he lost his life, overwhelmed by the odium
of the proceeding; different writers say by different modes
of death. I find in Fabius, far the most ancient writer,
that he lived even to old age; he states positively that, ad-

vanced in years, he made use of this phrase : "That exile
bore much heavier on the old man." The men of Rome
were not remiss in awarding their praises to the women, so
truly did they live without detracting from the merit of
others ; a temple was built also and dedicated to female
Fortune, to serve as a monument. The Volscians afterwards returned, in conjunction with the Æqui, into the
Roman territory ; but the Æqui would no longer have Attius Tullus as their leader ; hence from dispute, whether
the Volscians or the Æqui should give a general to the
allied army, a sedition, and afterwards a furious battle,
arose. There the good-fortune of the Roman people destroyed the two armies of the enemy, by a contest no less
bloody than obstinate. T. Sicinius and C. Aquillius were
made consuls. The Volscii fell as a province to Sicinius ;
the Hernici (for they too were in arms) to Aquillius. That
year the Hernici were defeated ; they came off with respect
to the Volscians on equal terms.

41. Sp. Cassius and Proculus Virginius were next made
consuls ; a treaty was struck with the Hernici ; two-thirds
of their land were taken from them : of this the consul Cassius was about to distribute one half among the Latins, the
other half among the commons. To this donation he was
adding a considerable portion of land, which, though public
property, he alleged was possessed by private individuals.
This proceeding alarmed several of the Senators, the actual
possessors, at the danger of their property ; the Senators
felt, moreover, a solicitude, on public grounds, that the
consul by his donation was establishing an influence dangerous to liberty. Then, for the first time, the Agrarian
law was proposed, which, even down to our own recollection, was never agitated without the greatest commotions in
the state. The other consul resisted the donation, the

Senators seconding him, nor were all the commons opposed
to him; they had at first begun to despise a gift which was
extended from citizens to allies : in the next place they frequently heard the consul Virginius in the assemblies, as it
were, prophesying—"that the gift of his colleague was
pestilential—that those lands were sure to bring slavery to
those who should receive them; that the way was paving
to a throne. For why was it that the allies were included,
and the Latin nation? What was the object of a third of
the land that had been taken being given back to the Hernici, so lately our enemies, except that, instead of Coriolanus being their leader, they may have Cassius?" The
dissuader and opposer of the agrarian law now began to be
popular. Both consuls then vied with each other in humor-
ing the commons. Virginius said that he would suffer the
lands to be assigned, provided they were assigned to no one
but to a Roman citizen. Cassius, because in the agrarian
donation he sought popularity among the allies, and was
therefore lowered in the estimation of his countrymen, in
order that by another donation he might conciliate their
affections, ordered that the money received for the Sicilian
corn should be refunded to the people. That, indeed, the
people rejected as nothing else than a present bribe for
regal authority; so strongly were his gifts spurned in the
minds of men, as if they possessed every thing in abundance, in consequence of their inveterate suspicions of his
aiming at sovereign power. As soon as he went out of
office, it is certain that he was condemned and put to death.
There are some who represent his father as the person who
inflicted the punishment; that he, having tried him at
home, scourged him and put him to death, and consecrated
his son's private property to Ceres; that out of this a
statue was set up and inscribed, "Given from the Cassian

family." In some authors I find it stated, and that is more probable, that a day of trial was assigned him for high treason, by the questors, Kæso Fabius and Lucius Valerius; and that he was condemned by the decision of the people; that his house was demolished by a public decree: this is the area before the Temple of Tellus. But whether that trial was private or public, he was condemned in the consulship of Ser. Cornelius and Q. Fabius.

42. The resentment of the people against Cassius was not of long duration. The allurements of the agrarian law, now that its proposer was gone, were of themselves gaining ground in their minds; and this feeling was further heightened by the parsimonious conduct of the Senators, who, the Volsci and Æqui having been defeated that year, defrauded the soldiers of the booty; whatever was taken from the enemy the consul Fabius sold, and lodged the proceeds in the treasury. The Fabian name was odious to the commons on account of the last consul: the Senate, however, succeeded in having Kæso Fabius elected consul with L. Æmilius. The commons, still further incensed at this, stirred up foreign war by exciting disturbance at home; civil dissensions were then interrupted by war. The Senators and commons uniting under the conduct of Æmilius, conquered in battle the Volsci and Æqui, who renewed hostilities. The retreat, however, destroyed more of the enemy than the battle, so perseveringly did the horse pursue them when routed. During the same year, on the ides of July, the temple of Castor was dedicated: it had been vowed during the Latin war in the dictatorship of Posthumius: his son, who was elected duumvir for that special purpose, dedicated it. In that year, also, the minds of the people were excited by the charms of the agrarian law. The tribunes of the people were for enhancing the popular power (vested in them) by

promoting the popular law. The Senators, considering that
there was enough and more than enough of frenzy in the
multitude, without any additional incitement, viewed with
horror largesses and all inducements to temerity : the Senators found in the consuls most energetic abettors in making
resistance.   That portion of the commonwealth, therefore,
prevailed ; and not for the present only, but for the forth-
coming year they succeeded in bringing in M. Fabius,
Kæso's brother, as consul and one still more detested by the
commons for his persecution of Sp. Cassius, L. Valerius.
In that year, also, there was a contest with the tribunes.
The law proved to be a vain project, and the abettors of the
law mere boasters, by their holding out a gift that was not
realized.   The Fabian name was from thence held in high
repute, after three successive consulates, and all, as it were,
uniformly exercised in contending with the tribunes ; accordingly, the honor remained for a considerable time in
that family, as being right well placed.   A Veientian war
was then commenced ; the Volscians, too, renewed hostilities ; but for foreign wars their strength was almost more
than sufficient, and they abused it by contending among
themselves.   To the distracted state of the public mind
were added prodigies from heaven, exhibiting almost daily
threats in the city and in the country ; and the soothsayers,
consulted by the state and by private individuals, one while
by means of entrails, another by birds, declared that there
was no other cause for divine anger but that the ceremonies
of religion were not duly attended to.   These terrors, however, terminated in this, that Oppia, a vestal virgin, being
found guilty of a breach of chastity, was made to suffer
punishment.

43. Quintus Fabius and C. Julius were then made consuls.
During this year the dissension at home was not abated,

and the war abroad was more desperate. Arms were taken
up by the Æquans; the Veientes also entered the territory
of the Romans, committing devastations; the solicitude
about which wars increasing, Kæso Fabius and Sp. Fusius
are created consuls. The Æqui were laying siege to Or-
tona, a Latin city. The Veientes, now satiated with plunder, threatened that they would besiege Rome itself. Which
terrors, when they ought to assuage, increased still further
the bad feelings of the commons; and the custom of de-
clining the military service was now returning, not of their
own accord; but Sp. Licinius, a tribune of the people,
thinking that the time was come for forcing the agrarian
law on the patricians by extreme necessity, had taken on
him the task of obstructing the military preparations. But
all the odium of the tribunitian power was turned on the
author; nor did the consuls rise up against him more zeal-
ously than his own colleagues; and by their assistance the
consuls hold the levy. An army is raised for the two wars
at the same time: one is given to Fabius to be led against
the Æqui, the other to Furius against the Veientians. And
with respect to the Veientians, nothing was done worthy of
mention. Fabius had much more trouble with his countrymen than with the enemy: that one man himself, as consul,
sustained the commonwealth, which the army was betraying, as far as in them lay, through their hatred of the consul. For when the consul, in addition to his other military
talents, which he exhibited amply in his preparations for
and conduct of war, had so drawn up his line that he
routed the enemy's army solely by a charge of his cavalry,
the infantry refused to pursue them when routed; and
though the exhortation of their general, whom they hated,
could not move them, neither could even their own infamy,
and the present public disgrace and subsequent danger, if

the enemy should recover courage, oblige them to quicken their pace, or even to stand in order of battle, if nothing else. Without orders they face about, and with a sorrowful air (you would suppose them beaten) they return to the camp, execrating at one time their general, at another time the services rendered by the cavalry. Nor were any remedies sought by the general for this so pestilent an example; so true is it that the most distinguished talents are more likely to be deficient in the tact of managing their countrymen than in that of conquering an enemy. The consul returned to Rome, not having so much increased his military glory as irritated and exasperated the hatred of his soldiers towards him. The patricians, however, succeeded in having the consulship remain in the Fabian family. They elect M. Fabius consul: Cn. Manlius is assigned as a colleague to Fabius.

44. This year also had a tribune as a proposer of the agrarian law. It was Titus Pontificius: he pursuing the same course, as, if it had succeeded with Sp. Licinius, obstructed the levy for a little time. The patricians being once more perplexed, Appius Claudius asserts "that the tribunitian power was put down last year; for the present by the very act, for the future by the precedent established, and since it was found that it could be rendered ineffective by its own strength; for that there never would be wanting a tribune who would both be willing to obtain a victory for himself over his colleague, and the favor of the better party by advancing the public weal. That both a plurality of tribunes, if there were need of such plurality, would be ready to assist the consuls; and that even one would be sufficient against all. Only let the consuls and leading members of the Senate take care to gain over, if not all, at least some of the tribunes, to the commonwealth and the Senate."

8 *

The Senators, convinced by the counsels of Appius, both collectively addressed the tribunes with kindness and civility, and the men of consular rank, according as each possessed personal influence over them individually, partly by conciliation, partly by authority, prevailed so far as to make them consent that the powers of the tribunitian office should be beneficial to the state; and, by the aid of four tribunes against one obstructor of the public good, the consuls complete the levy.   They then set out to the Veientian war, to which auxiliaries had flocked from all parts of Etruria, collected not so much for the sake of the Veientians as because they had formed a hope that the Roman state might be destroyed by internal discord.   And in the councils of all the states of Etruria the leading men openly stated "that the Roman power was eternal, unless they were distracted by disturbances among themselves.   That this was the only poison, this the bane discovered for powerful states, to render great empires mortal.   That this evil, a long time retarded, partly by the wise measures of the patricians, partly by the forbearance of the commons, had now proceeded to extremities.   That two states were now formed out of one; that each party had its own magistrates, its own laws.   That though at first they were accustomed to be turbulent during the levies, still that these same individuals had ever been obedient to their commanders during war; that military discipline being still retained, no matter what might be the state of the city, it had been possible to withstand the evil; that now the custom of not obeying their superior followed the Roman soldier even to the camp.   That in the last war, in the very field, in the very heat of battle, by consent of the army, the victory was voluntarily surrendered to the vanquished Æqui; that the standards were deserted, the general abandoned on the field, and that the army had re-

turned to the camp without orders.   That without doubt, if
perseverance were used, Rome might be conquered by her
own soldiery.   That nothing else was necessary than to declare and make a show of war; that the fates and the gods
would of themselves manage the rest."   These hopes had
armed the Etrurians, who in many vicissitudes had been
vanquished and victors.

45. The Roman consuls, also, dreaded nothing else than
their own strength and their own arms.   The recollection
of the destructive precedent set in the last war deterred
them from bringing matters to such a pass as that they
should have to fear two armies at the same time.   Accordingly they kept within their camp, avoiding this double
danger—"that delay and time itself would soften down resentment, and bring a right way of thinking to their minds.
The Veientian enemy and the Etrurians proceeded with so
much the greater precipitation; they provoked them to battle, first riding up to the camp and challenging them; at
length, when they produced no effect by reviling as well the
consuls themselves as the army, they stated, "that the pretense of internal dissension was assumed as a cloak for this
cowardice; and that the consuls distrusted as much the courage as the obedience of their soldiers.   That silence and in-
action among men in arms were a novel form of sedition."
Besides this they threw out reproaches, both true as well as
false, on the upstart quality of their race and origin.   While
they vociferated these reproaches beneath the very rampart
and gates, the consuls bore them without impatience; but at
one time indignation, at another time shame, distracted the
breasts of the ignorant multitude, and diverted their attention from intestine evils; they were unwilling that the
enemy should come off unpunished; they were unwilling
that success should accrue to the patricians or the consuls;

foreign and domestic hatred struggled for mastery in their breasts; at length the former prevail, so haughtily and insolently did the enemy revile them; they crowd in a body to the general's tent; they demand battle, they require that the signal be given. The consuls confer together as if to deliberate; they continue the conference for a long time; they were desirous of fighting, but that desire must be checked and concealed, that by opposition and delay they might increase the ardor of the soldiery once roused. An answer is returned, "that the matter in question was premature, that it was not yet time for fighting; that they should keep within their camp." They then issue a proclamation, "that they should abstain from fighting; that if any one fought without orders, they should punish him as an enemy." When they were thus dismissed, their eagerness for fighting increases in proportion as they think that the consuls were less disposed for it; the enemies, moreover, come up much more insolently, as soon as it was known that the consuls had determined not to fight. For they supposed "that they might insult them with impunity; that their arms were not intrusted to the soldiery. That the matter would explode in a violent mutiny; that a termination had come to the Roman empire." Relying on these hopes, they run up to the gates, heap reproaches on them, with difficulty refrain from assaulting the camp. Now, indeed, the Romans could no longer endure these insults; they crowd from every quarter of the camp to the consuls; they no longer, as formerly, make their demand with reserve, through the mediation of the centurions of the first rank; but all proceed indiscriminately with loud clamors. The affair was now ripe; still they put it off. Fabius then, his colleague giving way in consequence of his dread of mutiny being now augmented by the uproar, after he had com-

manded silence by sound of trumpet, says, "that these men
are able to conquer Cneius Manlius, I know ; that they are
willing, they themselves have prevented me from knowing.
It is, therefore, resolved and determined not to give the
signal unless they swear that they will return victorious
from this battle.   The soldier has once deceived the Roman
consul in the field, the gods he never will deceive."   There
was a centurion, Marcus Flavoleius, one of the foremost in
demanding battle ; he says : " M. Fabius, I will return victorious from the field."   If he deceived, he invokes the anger of Father Jove, Mars Gradivus, and of the other gods.
After him the entire army severally take the same oath.
The signal is given to them when sworn ; they take up
arms, go into battle, full of rage and of hope.   They bid
the Etrurians now to cast their reproaches ; they severally
require that the enemy, once so ready with the tongue,
should now stand before them armed as they were.   On that
day the bravery of all, both commons and patricians, was
extraordinary : the Fabian name, the Fabian race shone
forth most conspicuous ; they are determined to recover in
that battle the affections of the commons, which during
many civil contests had been alienated from them.   The
line of battle is formed ; nor do the Veientian foe and the
Etrurian legions decline the contest.

46. An almost certain hope was entertained that they
would no more fight with them than they had done with
the Æqui ; that even some more serious attempt was not to
be despaired of, considering the irritated state of their
feelings, and the very critical occasion.   The affair turned
out altogether differently ; for never before in any other
war did the Roman soldiers enter the field with more determined minds (so much had the enemy exasperated them by
taunts on the one hand, and the consuls by delay on the

other). The Etrurians had scarcely time to form their
ranks when, the javelins having been thrown away at ran-
dom, in the first hurry, rather than discharged with aim,
the battle had now come to close fighting, even to swords,
where the fury of war is most desperate. Among the foremost the Fabian family was distinguished for the sight it
afforded and the example it presented to their fellow-citizens ; one of these, Q. Fabius (he had been consul two years
before), as he was advancing at the head of his men against
a dense body of Veientians, and while engaged amidst numerous parties of the enemy, and therefore not prepared for
it, was transfixed with a sword through the breast by a Tuscan who presumed on his bodily strength and skill in arms :
on the weapon being extracted, Fabius fell forward on the
wound. Both armies felt the fall of this one man, and the
Roman began in consequence to give way, when the consul
Marcus Fabius leaped over the body as it lay, and, holding
up his buckler, said : "Is this what you swore, soldiers,
that you would return to the camp in flight? are you thus
more afraid of your most dastardly enemies than of Jupiter
and Mars, by whom you have sworn? But I who have not
sworn will either return victorious, or will fall fighting
here beside thee, Q. Fabius." Then Kæso Fabius, the consul of the preceding year, says to the consul : "Brother, is
it by these words you think you will prevail on them to
fight? the gods by whom they have sworn will prevail on
them. Let us also, as men of noble birth, as is worthy of
the Fabian name, enkindle the courage of the soldiers by
fighting rather than by exhorting." Thus the two Fabii
rush forward to the front with presented spears, and brought
on with them the whole line.

47. The battle being restored on one side, Cn. Manlius,
the consul, with no less ardor, encouraged the fight on the

other wing.   Where an almost similar result took place;
for, as the soldiers undauntedly followed Q. Fabius on the
one wing, so did they follow Manlius on this, as he was
driving the enemy now nearly routed; and when he, having
received a severe wound, retired from the battle, they fell
back, supposing that he was slain, and would have given
way, had not the other consul, galloping at full speed to
that quarter with some troops of horse, supported their
drooping energies, crying out that his colleague was still
alive, that he himself was now come victorious, having
routed the other wing.   Manlius also shows himself, to restore the battle.   The well-known voices of the two consuls
rekindle the courage of the soldiers; at the same time, too,
the enemy's line was now weakened, while, relying on their
superior numbers, they draw off their reserve and send them
to storm the camp.   This being assaulted without much resistance, while they lose time in attending to plunder rather
than to fighting, the Roman triarii,[1] who had not been able
to sustain the first shock, having sent an account to the consuls of the present position of affairs, return in a compact
body to the Prætorium, and of themselves renew the battle.
The consul Manlius also having returned to the camp, and
posted soldiers at all the gates, had blocked up every passage against the enemy.   This desperate situation aroused
the fury rather than the bravery of the Etrurians; for when
rushing on wherever hope held out the prospect of escape,
they had frequently advanced with fruitless efforts; one
body of young men makes an attack on the consul himself,
conspicuous from his arms.   The first weapons were intercepted by those who stood around him; afterwards their
force could not be sustained.   The consul falls, having re-

[1] The triarii were veteran soldiers of approved valor; they formed
the third line, whence their name.

ceived a mortal wound, and all around him are dispersed. The courage of the Etrurians rises. Terror drives the Romans in dismay through the entire camp; and matters would have come to extremities had not the lieutenant-generals, hastily seizing the body of the consul, opened a passage for the enemy at one gate. Through this they rush out; and, going away in the utmost disorder, they fall in with the other consul, who had been victorious; there, again, they are slain and routed in every direction. A glorious victory was obtained, saddened, however, by two so illustrious deaths. The consul, therefore, on the Senate voting him a triumph, replied that, "if the army could triumph without their general, he would readily accede to it in consideration of their distinguished behavior in that war; that for his own part, his family being plunged in grief in consequence of the death of his brother Q. Fabius, and the commonwealth being in some degree bereaved by the loss of one of her consuls, he would not accept the laurel blasted by public and private grief." The triumph thus resigned was more distinguished than any triumph actually enjoyed; so true it is that glory refused in due season sometimes returns with accumulated lustre. He next celebrates the two funerals of his colleague and brother, one after the other, he himself acting as panegyrist in the case of both, when, by ascribing to them his own deserts, he himself obtained the greatest share of them. And not unmindful of that which he had conceived at the commencement of his consulate, namely, the regaining the affection of the people, he distributes the wounded soldiers among the patricians to be cured. Most of them were given to the Fabii: nor were they treated with greater attention in any other place. From this time the Fabii began to be popular, and that not by any practices except such as were beneficial to the state.

48. Accordingly, Kæso Fabius, having been elected consul with T. Virginius, not more with the zealous wishes of
the Senators than of the commons, attended neither to
wars, nor levies, nor any other object, until, the hope of
concord being now in some measure commenced, the feelings of the commons might be consolidated with those of
the Senators as soon as possible.   Wherefore, at the commencement of the year, he proposed : "That before any
tribune should stand forth as an abettor of the agrarian law,
the patricians themselves should be beforehand with them
in performing their duty ; that they should distribute among
the commons the land taken from the enemy in as equal a
proportion as possible ; that it was but just that those should
obtain it by whose blood and sweat it was obtained."   The
patricians rejected the proposal with scorn ; some even complained that the once briliant talents of Kæso were now becoming wanton, and were waning through excess of glory.
There were afterwards no factions in the city.   The Latins
were harassed by the incursions of the Æqui.   Kæso being
sent thither with an army, passes into the very territory of
the Æqui to depopulate it.   The Æqui retired into the
towns, and kept themselves within the walls : on that account no battle worth mentioning was fought.   But a blow
was received from the Veientian foe through the temerity
of the other consul ; and the army would have been all cut
off, had not Kæso Fabius come to their assistance in time.
From that time their was neither peace nor war with the
Veientians; their proceedings had now come very near to
the form of that of brigands.   They retired from the Roman
troops into the city; when they perceived that the troops
were drawn off, they made incursions into the country, alternately evading war by quiet, quiet by war.   Thus the matter could neither be dropped altogether nor brought to a

conclusion ; and other wars were impending either at the
moment, as from the Æqui and Volsci, who remained in-
active no longer than until the recent smart of their late
disaster should pass away ; or it was evident that the Sabines,
ever hostile, and all Etruria would put themselves in motion ; but the Veientians, a constant rather than a formidable enemy, kept their minds in constant uneasiness by their
insults more frequently than by any danger apprehended
from them ; a matter which could at no time be neglected,
and which suffered them not to direct their attention to any
other object.   Then the Fabian family addressed the Senate ; the consul speaks in the name of the family : " Conscript fathers, the Veientian war requires, as you know, a
constant rather than a strong force.   Do you attend to other
wars ; assign the Fabii as enemies to the Veientians.   We
pledge ourselves that the majesty of the Roman name shall
be safe in that quarter.   That war, as the property of our
family, it is our determination to conduct at our own private expense.   Let the republic be spared the expense of
soldiers and money there."   The warmest thanks were returned to them.   The consul, leaving the Senate-house,
accompanied by the Fabii in a body, who had been standing
in the porch of the Senate-house, returned home.   Being
ordered to attend on the following day in arms at the consul's gate, they retire to their homes.

49. The rumor spreads through the entire city ; they
extol the Fabii to the skies by their enconiums.   "That a
single family had taken on them the burden of the state ;
that the Veientian war had now become a private concern, a
private quarrel.   If there were two families of the same
strength in the city, let them demand, the one the Volsci
for itself, the other the Æqui ; that all the neighboring
states might be subdued, the Roman people all the time en-

joying profound peace." The day following, the Fabii take up arms; they assemble where they had been ordered. The consul coming forth in his paludamentum,[1] beholds his entire family in the porch drawn up in order of march; being received into the centre, he orders the standards to be carried forward. Never did an army march through the city either smaller in number or more distinguished in fame and in the admiration of all men. Three hundred and six soldiers, all patricians, all of the one stock, not one of whom the Senate would reject as a leader in its palmiest days, proceeded on their march, menacing destruction to the Veientian state by the prowess of a single family. A crowd followed, partly belonging to their kinsmen and friends, who contemplated in mind no moderation either as to their hopes or anxiety, but every thing on the highest scale; partly consisting of individuals not connected with their family, aroused by solicitude for the public weal, all enraptured with esteem and admiration. They bid them " proceed in the brave resolve, proceed with happy omens, bring back results proportioned to their undertaking: thence to expect consulships and triumphs, all rewards, all honors from them." As they passed the Capitol and the citadel, and the other sacred edifices, they offer up prayers to all the gods that presented themselves to their sight or to their mind; that "they would send forward that band with prosperity and success, and soon send them back safe into their country to their parents." In vain were these prayers sent up. Having set out on their luckless road by the right-hand postern of the Carmental gate, they arrive at the River

---

[1] Before a consul set out on any expedition, he offered sacrifices and prayers in the Capitol; and then, laying aside his consular gown, marched out of the city dressed in a military robe of state, called Paludamentum.

Cremera : this appeared a favorable situation for fortifying a post. L. Æmilius and C. Servilius were then created consuls.   And as long as there was nothing else to occupy them but mutual devastations, the Fabii were not only sufficiently able to protect their garrison, but through the entire tract, as far as the Etrurian joins the Roman territory, they protected all their own districts and ravaged those of the enemy, spreading their forces along both frontiers.   There was afterwards an intermission, though not of long duration, to these depredations : while both the Veientians, having sent for an army from Etruria, assault the post at the Cremera, and the Roman troops, led thither by L. Æmilius the consul, come to a close engagement in the field with the Etrurians ; although the Veientians had scarcely time to draw up their line : for during the first alarm, while the ranks are posting themselves behind their respective banners and they are stationing their reserves, a brigade of Roman cavalry, charging them suddenly in flank, took away all opportunity not only of commencing the fight, but even of standing their ground.   Thus, being driven back to the Red Rocks (there they pitched their camp), they suppliantly sue for peace ; for the obtaining of which they were sorry, from the natural inconsistency of their minds, before the Roman garrison was drawn off from the Cremera.

50. Again, the Veientian state had to contend with the Fabii without any additional military armament [on either side]; and there were not merely incursions into each other's territories, or sudden attacks on those making the incursions, but they fought repeatedly in the open field and in pitched battles ; and one family of the Roman people oftentimes gained the victory over an entire Etrurian state, one of the most powerful at that time.   This at first appeared mortifying and humiliating to the Veientians ; then (they formed)

a design, suggested by the circumstance, of surprising their
daring enemy by an ambuscade ; they were even glad that
the confidence of the Fabii was increasing by their great
success.   Wherefore cattle were frequently driven in the
way of the plundering parties, as if they had come there
by mere accident, and tracts of land were abandoned by the
flight of the peasants ; and troops of armed men sent to
prevent the devastations retreated more frequently from
pretended than from real fear.   And now the Fabii had
such a contempt for the enemy, as to believe that their in-
vincible arms could not be withstood either in any place or
on any occasion : this presumption carried them so far that,
at the sight of some cattle at a distance from Cremera, with
an extensive plain lying between, they ran down to it
(although few troops of the enemy were observed) ; and
when incautious and in disorderly haste they had passed
the ambuscade placed on either side of the very road ; and
when dispersed in different directions they began to carry
off the cattle straying about, as is usual when they are
frightened, the Veientians rise up suddenly from their ambuscade, and the enemy were in front and on every side.
At first the shout that was raised terrified them ; then weapons assailed them from every side ; and, the Etrurians
closing, they also were compelled, hemmed in as they now
were, by a compact body of soldiers, to contract their own
circle within a narrower compass ; which circumstance rendered striking both their own paucity of numbers, and the
superior numbers of the enemy, the ranks being crowded in
a narrow space.   Then the plan of fighting, which they had
directed equally against every part, being now relinquished,
they all incline their forces towards one point ; in that direction straining every effort, both with their bodies and
arms, they forced a passage by forming a wedge.   The way

led to a hill of moderate acclivity; here they first halted:
presently, as soon as the higher ground afforded them time
to gain breath, and to recover from so great a panic, they
repulsed them as they advanced up; and the small band, by
the advantage of the ground, was gaining the victory, had
not a party of the Veientians, sent round the ridge of the hill,
made their way to the summit; thus again the enemy obtained the higher ground; all the Fabii were killed to a
man, and the fort was taken: it is agreed on all hands that
the three hundred and six were cut off; that one[1] only,
who nearly attained the age of puberty, was left as a stock
for the Fabian race; and that he was destined to prove the
greatest support in the dangerous emergencies of the Roman
people, both at home and in war.

51. At the time when this disaster was received, C. Horatius and T. Menenius were consuls.   Menenius was immediately sent against the Etrurians, elated with victory.   Then
too an unsuccessful battle was fought, and the enemy took
possession of the Janiculum; and the city would have been
besieged, scarcity of provisions bearing hard upon them in
addition to the war (for the Etrurians had passed the Tiber),
had not the consul Horatius been recalled from the Volsci;
and so closely did that war approach the very walls, that
the first battle was fought near the Temple of Hope with
doubtful success, and a second time at the Colline gate.
There, although the Romans had the advantage in a slight
degree only, yet that contest rendered the soldiers better
for future battles by restoring to them their former courage.
Aulus Virginius and Sp. Servilius are created consuls.
After the defeat sustained in the last battle, the Veientians
declined an engagement.   Ravages were committed, and

---

[1] This statement is rejected by Niebuhr entirely.

they made incursions in every direction on the Roman territory from the Janiculum, as if from a fortress; nowhere
were the cattle or the husbandmen safe.   They were afterwards entrapped by the same stratagem as that by which
they had entrapped the Fabii: having pursued some cattle
that had been driven on designedly for the purpose of de-
coying them, they fell into an ambuscade; in proportion as
they were more numerous, the slaughter was greater.   The
violent resentment resulting from this disaster was the cause
and commencement of one still greater; for, having crossed
the Tiber by night, they attempted to assault the camp of
the consul Servilius; being repulsed from thence with great
slaughter, they with difficulty made good their retreat into
the Janiculum.   The consul himself also crosses the Tiber,
fortifies his camp at the foot of the Janiculum: at break of
day on the following morning, both from being somewhat
elated by the success of the battle of the day before, more,
however, because the scarcity of corn forced him into measures which, though dangerous (he adopted), because they
were more expeditious, he rashly marched his army up the
steep of the Janiculum to the camp of the enemy, and being
repulsed from thence with more disgrace than he had repulsed them on the preceding day, he was saved, both himself and his army, by the intervention of his colleague.
The Etrurians (hemmed in), between the two armies, when
they presented their rear to the one and the other by turns,
were entirely cut off.   Thus the Veientian war was crushed
by a fortunate act of temerity.

52. Together with the peace, provisions returned to the
city in greater abundance, both by reason of corn having
been brought in from Campania, and, as soon as the fear
felt by each of future famine left them, that corn being
brought forward which had been hoarded up.   Then their

minds once more became licentious from their present
abundance and ease, and their former subjects of complaint,
now that there were none abroad, they sought for at home;
the tribunes began to excite the commons by their poison,
the agrarian law: they roused them against the Senators
who opposed it, and not only against them as a body, but
also against particular individuals. Q. Considius and T.
Genucius, the proposers of the agrarian law, appoint a day
of trial for T. Menenius: the loss of the fort of Cremera,
while the consul had his standing camp at no great distance
from thence, was the charge against him.   They crushed
him, though both the Senators had exerted themselves in
his behalf with no less earnestness than in behalf of Coriolanus, and the popularity of his father Agrippa was not yet
forgotten.   The tribunes, however, went no further than a
fine: though they had arraigned him for a capital offense,
they imposed on him, when found guilty, a fine of two
thousand *asses*.   This proved fatal.   They say that he could
not submit to the disgrace, and to the anguish of mind (occasioned by it); that, in consequence, he was taken off by
disease.   Another Senator, Sp. Servilius, being soon after
arraigned, as soon as he went out of office, a day of trial
having been appointed for him by the tribunes, L. Cædicius
and T. Statius, at the very commencement of the year, in
the consulship of C. Nautius and P. Valerius, did not, like
Menenius, meet the attacks of the tribunes with supplica-
tions from himself and the patricians, but with firm reli-
ance on his own integrity, and his personal influence.   The
battle with the Etrurians at the Janiculum was the charge
against him also; but, being a man of an intrepid spirit, as
he had formerly acted in the case of public peril, so now,
in that which was personal to himself, he dispelled the
danger by boldly facing it, by confuting not only the tri-

bunes but the commons also, by a bold speech, and upbraid-
ing them with the condemnation and death of T. Menenius,
by the good offices of whose father the commons were formerly re-established, and were now in possession of those laws
and those magistrates, by means of which they then exercised their insolence; his colleague Virginius also, who was
brought forward as a witness, aided him by assigning to
him a share of his own deserts; the condemnation of Menenius, however, was of greater service to him (so much had
they changed their minds).

53. The contests at home were now concluded. A Veientian war broke out, with whom the Sabines had united
their forces. The consul P. Valerius, after auxiliaries were
sent for from the Latins and Hernicians, being dispatched
to Veii with an army, immediately attacks the Sabine camp,
which had been pitched before the walls of their allies;
and occasioned such great consternation, that while, dispersed in different directions, they sally forth to repel the
assault of the enemy, the gate which the Romans first attacked was taken; then within the rampart there was rather
a carnage than a battle. From the camp the alarm spreads
into the city; the Veientians run to arms in as great a
panic as if Veii had been taken: some come up to the support of the Sabines, others fall upon the Romans, who had
directed all their force against the camp. For a little while
they were disconcerted and thrown into confusion; then
they too, forming two fronts, make a stand; and the cavalry, being commanded by the consul to charge, routs the
Etrurians and puts them to flight; and in the same hour
two armies and two of the most influential and powerful of
the neighboring states were vanquished. While these transactions are going on at Veii, the Volsci and Æqui had
pitched their camp in the Latin territory, and laid waste

9

their frontiers. The Latins, by their own exertions, being joined by the Hernicians, without either a Roman general or Roman auxiliaries, stripped them of their camp. Besides recovering their own effects, they obtained immense booty. The consul C. Nautius, however, was sent against the Volsci from Rome. The custom, I suppose, was not pleasing for allies to carry on wars with their own forces and under their own direction without a Roman general and troops. There was no kind of injury or indignity that was not practised against the Volsci ; nor could they be prevailed on, however, to come to an engagement in the field.

54. Lucius Furius and Caius Manlius were the next consuls. The Veientians fell to Manlius as his province. War, however, did not take place ; a truce for forty years was granted them at their request, corn and pay for the soldiers being demanded of them. Disturbance at home immediately succeeds to peace abroad : the commons were goaded by the tribunes with the excitement of the agrarian law. The consuls, nothing intimidated by the condemnation of Menenius, nor by the danger of Servilius, resist with their utmost might ; Cn. Genucius, a tribune of the people, arraigned the consuls on their going out of office. Lucius Æmilius and Opiter Virginius enter on the consulate. Instead of Virginius I find Vopiscus Julius consul in some annals. In this year (whatever consuls it had) Furius and Manlius, being summoned to trial before the people, go about in suppliant garb, not more to the commons than to the younger patricians ; they advise, they caution them, "to keep themselves from honors and the administration of public affairs, and that they would consider the consular fasces, the prætexta, and curule chair, as nothing else than the decorations of a funeral ; that when covered with these

fine insignia, as with fillets, they were doomed to death.
But if the charms of the consulate were so great, they
should rest satisfied that the consulate was held in captivity and crushed by the tribunitian power; that everything was to be done at the nod and command of the tribune
by the consul, as if he were a tribune's beadle.   If he stir,
if he have reference to the patricians, if he should think
for a moment that there existed any other party in the
state but the commons, let him place before his eyes the
banishment of Caius Marcius, the condemnation and death
of Menenius." Fired by these discourses, the patricians
from that time held their consultations not in public, but in
private, and withdrawn from the knowledge of the many;
where, when this one point was agreed on, that the accused
must be rescued, whether by just or unjust means, every
proposition that was most desperate was most approved;
nor was an actor wanted for any deed, however daring.
Accordingly, on the day of trial, when the people stood in
the Forum in anxious expectation, they at first began to
feel surprised that the tribune did not come down; then,
when the delay was now becoming more suspicious, they
considered that he was deterred by the nobles, and they
complained that the public cause was abandoned and betrayed.   At length those who had been waiting before the
gate of the tribune's residence bring word that he was found
dead in his house.   As soon as rumor spread this through
the whole assembly, just as an army disperses on the fall of
its general, so did they separate in different directions. The
principal panic seized the tribunes, now warned by their
colleague's death what little aid the devoting laws afforded
them.   Nor did the patricians bear their joy with sufficient
moderation ; and so far was any of them from feeling com-
punction at the guilty act, that even those who were inno-

cent wished to be considered to have perpetrated it, and it was openly declared that the tribunitian power should be subdued by chastisement.

55. Immediately after this victory of a most ruinous precedent a levy is proclaimed; and the tribunes being now overawed, the consuls accomplish the matter without any opposition. Then, indeed, the commons became enraged more on account of the silence of the tribunes than the command of the consuls; and they said "there was an end of their liberty; that they were come back again to the old condition of things; that the tribunitian power had died along with Genucius and was buried with him; that other means must be devised and practised by which to resist the patricians; and that the only method for that was that the people should defend themselves, since they now had no other aid. That four-and-twenty lictors waited on the consuls; and that these very individuals were from among the commons; that nothing could be more despicable, nor weaker, if there were only persons who could despise them; that each person magnified those things, and made them objects of terror to himself." When they had excited each other by these discourses, a lictor was dispatched by the consuls to Volero Publilius, a man belonging to the commons, because he stated that, having been a centurion, he ought not to be made a common soldier. Volero appeals to the tribunes. When one came to his assistance, the consuls order the man to be stripped and the rods to be got ready. "I appeal to the people," says Volero, "since tribunes had rather see a Roman citizen scourged before their eyes than themselves be butchered by you in their bed." The more vehemently he cried out, the more violently did the lictor tear off his clothes and strip him. Then Volero, being both himself of great bodily strength,

and being aided by his partisans, having repulsed the lictor, when the shouts of those indignant in his behalf became very intense, betook himself into the thickest part of the crowd, crying out, "I appeal, and implore the protection of the commons ; assist me, fellow-citizens ; assist me, fellow-soldiers; there is no use in waiting for the tribunes, who themselves stand in need of your aid." The men, being much excited, prepare as it were for battle ; and it became manifest that there was urgent danger, that nothing would be held sacred by any one, that there would no longer exist any public or private right. When the consuls faced this so violent storm, they soon experienced that majesty without strength had but little security ; the lictors being maltreated, the fasces broken, they are driven from the Forum into the Senate-house, uncertain how far Volero would push his victory. After that, the disturbance subsiding, when they had ordered the Senate to be convened, they complain of the outrages committed on themselves, of the violence of the people, the daring of Volero. Many violent measures having been proposed, the elder members prevailed, who recommended that the unthinking rashness of the commons should not be met by the passionate resentment of the patricians.

56. The commons having espoused the interest of Volero, with great warmth choose him, at the next election, tribune of the people for that year, which had Lucius Pinarius and Publius Furius for consuls ; and, contrary to the opinion of all men, who thought that he would let loose his tribuneship in harassing the consuls of the preceding year, postponing private resentment to the public interest, without assailing the consuls even by a single word, he proposed a law to the people that plebeian magistrates should be elected at the comitia by tribes. A matter of no trifling moment

was now being brought forward, under an aspect at first
sight by no means alarming; but one which in reality deprived the patricians of all power to elect whatever tribunes
they pleased by the suffrages of their clients. The patricians used all their energies in resisting this proposition,
which was most pleasing to the commons; and though none
of the college could be induced, by the influence either of
the consuls or of the chief members of the Senate, to enter
a protest against it, the only means of resistance which now
existed, yet the matter, important as it was by its own
weight, is spun out by contention till the following year.
The commons re-elect Volero as tribune. The Senators,
considering that the question would be carried to the very
extreme of a struggle, elect to the consulate Appius Claudius, the son of Appius, who was both hated by and hated
the commons, ever since the contests between them and his
father. Titus Quintius is assigned to him as his colleague.
In the very commencement of the year no other question
took precedence of that regarding the law. But though
Volero was the inventor of it, his colleague, Lætorius, was
both a more recent abettor of it, as well as a more energetic
one. While Volero confined himself to the subject of the
law, avoiding all abuse of the consuls, he commenced with
accusing Appius and his family, as having ever been most
overbearing and cruel towards the Roman commons, contending that he had been elected by the Senators, not as
consul, but as executioner, to 'harass and torture the people;
his rude tongue, he being a military man, was not sufficient
to express the freedom of his sentiments. Language therefore
failing him, he says: "Romans, since I do not speak with
as much readiness as I make good what I have spoken, attend
here to-morrow. I will either die here before your eyes, or
will carry the law." On the following day the tribunes

take possession of the temple ; the consuls and the nobility take their places in the assembly to obstruct the law. Lætorius orders all persons to be removed except those going to vote; the young nobles kept their places, paying no regard to the officer ; then Lætorius orders some of them to be seized. The consul Appius insisted "that the tribune had no jurisdiction over any one except a plebeian ; for that he was not a magistrate of the people in general, but only of the commons ; for that even he himself could not, according to the usage of their ancestors, by virtue of his authority remove any person ; because the words run thus, *if ye think proper, depart, Romans.*" He was able to disconcert Lætorius by arguing fluently and contemptuously concerning the right. The tribune, therefore, burning with rage, sends his beadle to the consul ; the consul sends his lictor to the tribune, exclaiming that he was a private individual, without power and without magistracy ; and the tribune would have been roughly treated, had not both the entire assembly risen up with great warmth in behalf of the tribune against the consul, and a rush of persons be· longing to the multitude, which was now much excited, taken place from the entire city into the Forum. Appius, however, withstood so great a storm with obstinacy, and the contest would have ended in a battle, not without blood, had not Quintius, the other consul, after giving it in charge to the men of consular dignity to remove his colleague from the Forum by force, if they could not do it otherwise, himself assuaged the enraged people by entreaties, and implored the tribunes to dismiss the assembly. "That they should give their passion time to cool; that delay would not deprive them of their power, but would add prudence to strength ; and that the Senators would be under the control of the people, and the consul under that of the Senators."

57. With difficulty the people were pacified by Quintius; with much more difficulty was the other consul by the patricians. The assembly of the people being at length dismissed, the consuls convene the Senate; where, though fear and resentment by turns had produced a diversity of opinions, the more they were recalled, after the lapse of time, from violence to reflection, the more averse did they become to a continuance of the dispute, so that they returned thanks to Quintius, because by his exertions the disturbance had been quieted. Appius is requested "to consent that the consular dignity should be merely so great as it could be in a peaceably conducted state; that as long as the tribune and consuls were drawing all power, each to his own side, no strength was left between; that the object aimed at was in whose hands the commonwealth should be, distracted and torn as it was, rather than that it should be safe." Appius, on the contrary, called gods and men to witness that "the commonwealth was betrayed and abandoned through cowardice; that it was not the consul that was wanting to the Senate, but the Senate to the consul; that more oppressive laws were now being submitted to than were sanctioned on the sacred mount." Overcome, however, by the unanimous feeling of the Senators, he desisted: the law is carried without opposition.

58. Then for the first time the tribunes were elected in the comitia by tribes. Piso said that three were added to the number, whereas there had been only two before. He names the tribunes also—Caius Sicinius, Lucius Numitorius, Marcus Duilius, Spurius Icilius, Lucius Mecilius. During the disturbance at Rome a war with the Volscians and Æquans broke out; they had laid waste the lands, so that if any secession of the people should take place, they might find a refuge with them. The differences being afterwards set-

tled, they removed their camp backward. Appius Claudius
was sent against the Volscians ; the Æquans fell to Quintius
as his province. The severity of Appius was the same in
war as at home, being more unrestrained because he was
free from tribunitian control. He hated the commons with
more than his father's hatred : he had been defeated by
them ; when he was set up as the only consul to oppose the
tribunitian influence, a law was passed, which former consuls obstructed with less effort, amidst hopes of the Senators
by no means so great (as those formed of him). His resentment and indignation at this excited his imperious temper
to harass the army by the rigor of his command ; nor could
it (the army), however, be subdued by any means, such a
spirit of opposition had they imbibed. They executed
every measure slowly, indolently, negligently, and with
stubbornness : neither shame nor fear restrained them. If
he wished the army to move on with expedition, they designedly went more slowly ; if he came up to them to encourage them in their work, they all relaxed the energy
which they before exerted of their own accord ; when he
was present, they cast down their eyes, they silently cursed
him as he passed by ; so that his mind, invulnerable to plebeian hatred, was sometimes moved. All kind of harsh
treatment being tried in vain, he no longer held any intercourse with the soldiers ; he said the army was corrupted
by the centurions ; he sometimes gibingly called them tribunes of the people and Voleros.

59. None of these circumstances were unknown to the
Volscians, and they pressed on with so much the more
vigor, hoping that the Roman army would entertain the
same spirit of opposition against Appius which they had
formerly entertained against the consul Fabius. But they
were much more violent against Appius than against Fa-

9 *

bius. For they were not only unwilling to conquer, like
Fabius's army, but they wished to be conquered. When
led out to the field, they made for their camp in an ignominious flight; nor did they stand their ground until
they saw the Volscians advancing to their fortifications, and
making dreadful havoc on the rear of their army. Then
the obligation to fight was wrung from them, in order that
the victorious enemy should be dislodged from their lines;
yet it was sufficiently plain that the Roman soldiers were
only unwilling that their camp should be taken; some of
them gloried in their own defeat and disgrace. When the
determined spirit of Appius, undaunted by these things,
wished to exercise severity still farther, and he summoned
a meeting, the lieutenant-generals and tribunes flock around
him, advising him "that he would not determine on venturing a trial of an authority the entire strength of which
lay in the acquiescence of those who were to obey. That
the soldiers generally refused to come to the assembly, and
that their clamors were heard in every direction demanding
that the camp should be removed from the Volscian territory. That the victorious enemy were but a little time ago
almost at the very gates and rampart; and that not merely
a suspicion, but a manifest indication of a grevious disaster,
presented itself to their eyes." Yielding at length (since
they would gain nothing save a delay of punishment), having prorogued the assembly, after he had given orders that
their march should be proclaimed for the following day, he,
at the first dawn, gave the signal for departure by sound of
trumpet. When the army, having just got clear of the
camp, were forming themselves, the Volscians, as being
aroused by the same signal, fall upon those in the rear;
from whom the alarm spreading to the van, confounded
both the battalions and ranks with such consternation, that

neither the generals' orders could be distinctly heard nor
the lines be drawn up, no one thinking of any thing but
flight. In such confusion did they make their way through
heaps of dead bodies and of arms, that the enemy ceased to
pursue sooner than the Romans to fly. The soldiers being
at length collected from their scattered rout, the consul,
after he had in vain followed his men for the purpose of
rallying them, pitched his camp in a peaceful part of the
country ; and an assembly being convened, after inveighing,
not without good reason, against the army as traitors to
military discipline, deserters of their posts, frequently asking them, one by one, where were their standards, where
their arms ; he first beat with rods and then beheaded those
soldiers who had thrown down their arms, the standard-
bearers who had lost their standards, and moreover the centurions, and those with the double allowance, who had left
their ranks. With respect to the rest of the multitude,
every tenth man was drawn by lot for punishment.

60. In a contrary manner to this, the consul and soldiers
in the country of the Æquans vied with each other in cour-
tesy and acts of kindness : both Quintius was naturally
milder in disposition, and the ill-fated severity of his colleague caused him to indulge more in his own good temper.
This, such great cordiality between the general and his
army, the Æquans did not venture to meet ; they suffered
the enemy to go through their lands committing devastations in every direction. Nor were depredations committed
more extensively in that quarter in any preceding war.
Praises were also added, in which the minds of soldiers find
no less pleasure than in rewards. The army returned more
reconciled both to their general, and also on account of the
general to the patricians ; stating that a parent was assigned
to them, a master to the other army by the Senate. The

year now passed, with varied success in war, and furious
dissensions at home and abroad, was rendered memorable
chiefly by the elections by tribes ; the matter was more important from the victory in the contest entered into, than
from any real advantage ; for there was more of dignity ab-
stracted from the elections themselves by the exclusion of
the patricians, than there was influence either added to the
commons or taken from the patricians.

61. A more turbulent year[1] next followed, Lucius Valerius, Tiberius Æmilius being consuls, both by reason of the
struggles between the different orders concerning the agrarian law, as well as on account of the trial of Appius
Claudius ; for whom, as a most active opposer of the law,
and as one who supported the cause of the possessors of the
public land, as if a third consul, Marcus Duilius and Caius
Sicinius appointed a day of trial.[2] Never before was an
accused person so hateful to the commons brought to trial
before the people ; overwhelmed with their resentment on
his own account,[3] and also on account of his father.   The
patricians too seldom made equal exertions in behalf of any
one : "That the champion of the Senate, and the asserter
of their dignity, opposed to all the storms of the tribunes
and commons, was exposed to the resentment of the commons, merely for having exceeded bounds in the contest."
Appius Claudius himself was the only one of the patricians

---

[1] Niebuhr. ii. p. 231, thinks that it was in this year the Icilian law
was passed, according to which any person interrupting the proceedings of the tribunes rendered himself liable to capital punishment.
—*Twiss.*

[2] Several charges were brought against Appius, according to Dion.
ix. 54, who also states that he did not die of any disease, but that he
laid violent hands on himself.—*Ruperti.*

[3] The original has *plenus suarum—irarum ;* that is, the anger not of
Appius against the commons, but of the commons against him.

who made light both of the tribunes and commons and his
own trial. Neither the threats of the commons nor the
entreaties of the Senate could ever persuade him not only
to change his garb, or address persons as a suppliant, but
not even so far as to soften or relax any thing from the usual
asperity of his style, when his cause was to be pleaded before
the people. The expression of his countenance was the
same ; the same stubbornness in his looks, the same spirit
of pride in his language ; so that a great part of the commons felt no less awe of Appius when arraigned than they
had felt of him when consul. He pleaded his cause once,
and with the same spirit of an accuser which he had been
accustomed to adopt on all occasions ; and he so far astounded
both the tribunes and the commons by his intrepidity, that,
of their own accord, they posponed the day of trial ; then
they allowed the matter to be protracted. Nor was the time
now very distant ; before, however, the appointed day came,
he dies of some disease ; and when the tribunes of the people
endeavored to impede his funeral panegyric,[1] the commons
would not allow that the last day of so great a man should
be defrauded of the usual honors ; and they listened to the
panegyric of him when dead with as patient ears as they
had listened to the charges brought against him when
living, and attended his funeral in vast numbers.

62. In the same year the consul Valerius, having marched
an army against the Æquans, when he could not entice the
enemy to an engagement, set about assaulting their camp.
A violent storm sent down from heaven, with thunder and
hail, prevented him. Then, on a signal for a retreat being

---

[1] Conf. Nieb. ii. n. 754. It may be well to mention that Niebuhr
considered that this account regarding the death of Appius was all
fictitious. The Greek writers, scil. Dion. ix. 54, Zonar. vii. 17, state
that he laid violent hands on himself.

given, their surprise was excited by the return of such fair weather, that they felt a scruple a second time to attack a camp which was defended, as it were, by some divine power ; all the rage of war was turned on the devastation of the land.   The other consul, Æmilius, conducted the war against the Sabines.   There also, because the enemy confined themselves within their walls, the lands were laid waste.   Then, by the burning not only of the country-houses, but of the villages also, which were thickly inhabited, the Sabines being aroused, after they met the depredators, on retreating from an engagement left undecided, on the following day removed their camp into a safer situation. This seemed a sufficient reason to the consul why he should leave the enemy as conquered, departing thence, the war being still unfinished.

63. During these wars, while dissensions still continued at home, Titus Numicius Priscus, Aulus Virginius, were elected consuls.   The commons appeared determined no longer to brook a delay of the agrarian law, and extreme violence was on the eve of being resorted to, when it was ascertained from the burning of the country-houses and the flight of the peasants that the Volscians were at hand : this circumstance checked the sedition that was now ripe and almost breaking out.   The consuls, having been instantly forced to the war by the Senate,[1] after leading forth the youth from the city, rendered the rest of the commons more quiet.   And the enemy indeed, having done nothing else except alarming the Romans by groundless fear, depart with great precipitation.   Numicius marched to Antium against the Volscians, Virginius against the Æquans.   Here a signal

---

[1] In the original we read *coacti extemplo ab senatu.* Niebuhr considers this reading to be corrupt, and is satisfied that the correct reading is *coacto extemplo senatu.* See ii. n. 555.

overthrow being well-nigh received from an ambuscade, the bravery of the soldiers restored (the Roman) superiority, which had been endangered through the carelessness of the consul. The general conducted affairs better against the Volscians. The enemy were routed in the first engagement, and forced to fly into the city of Antium, a very wealthy place considering those times; the consul, not venturing to attack it, took from the people of Antium another town, Ceno, which was by no means so wealthy. While the Æquans and Volscians engage the attention of the Roman armies, the Sabines advanced in their devastations even to the gates of the city; then they themselves, a few days after, received from the two armies heavier losses than they had occasioned, the two consuls having entered their territories under exasperated feelings.

64. Towards the close of the year there was some peace, but, as frequently at other times, disturbed by contests between the patricians and commons. The exasperated commons refused to attend the consular elections: Titus Quintius, Quintus Servilius, were elected consuls by the patricians and their dependents: the consuls have a year similar to the preceding, the commencement embroiled, and afterwards tranquil by external war. The Sabines marching across the plains of Crustuminum with great rapidity, after carrying fire and sword along the banks of the Anio, being repulsed when they had come up nearly to the Colline gate and the walls, drove off, however, great booty of men and cattle: the consul Servilius, having pursued them with a determined army, was unable to come up with the main body itself on the champaign country; he carried his devastation, however, so extensively, that he left nothing unmolested by war, and returned after obtaining plunder much exceeding that carried off by the enemy. The public interest was sup-

ported extremely well against the Volscians also, by the exertions as well of the general as of the soldiers. First they
fought a pitched battle, on equal ground, with great slaughter and much bloodshed on both sides ; and the Romans,
because the fewness of their numbers was more likely to
make the loss felt, would have given way, had not the consul, by a well-timed fiction, reanimated the army, crying out
that the enemy were flying on the other wing ; making a
charge, they, by supposing that they were victorious, became
so. The consul fearing lest, by pressing too far, he might
renew the contest, gave the signal for a retreat. A few days
intervened, rest being taken on both sides as if by a tacit
suspension of arms ; during these days a vast number of
persons from all the states of the Volscians and Æquans
came to the camp, certain that the Romans would depart
during the night if they should perceive them. Accordingly, about the third watch they come to attack the camp.
Quintius, having allayed the confusion which the sudden
panic had occasioned, after ordering the soldiers to remain
quiet in their tents, leads out a cohort of the Hernicians for
an advance guard : the trumpeters and horneteers he mounts
on horseback, and commands them to sound their trumpets
before the rampart, and to keep the enemy in suspense till
daylight : during the rest of the night every thing was so
quiet in the camp, that the Romans had even the advantage
of sleep. The sight of the armed infantry, whom they both
considered to be more numerous than they were, and to be Romans, the bustle and neighing of the horses, which became
restless, both from the strange riders placed on them, and,
moreover, from the sound of the trumpets frightening them,
kept the Volscians intently awaiting an attack of the enemy.

65. When day dawned, the Romans, invigorated and re-
freshed with sleep, on being marched out to battle, at the

first onset overpowered the Volscians, wearied from standing and want of rest ; though the enemy rather retired than
were routed, because in the rear there were hills to which
there was a secure retreat, the ranks behind the first line
being unbroken.   The consul, when they came to the un-
even ground, halts his army ; the soldiers were kept back
with difficulty : they cried out and demanded to be allowed
to pursue the enemy, now discomfited.   The calvary,
crowding around the general, proceed more violently : they
cry out that they would proceed before the first line.
While the consul hesitates, relying on the valor of his men,
yet having little confidence in the place, they all cry out
that they would proceed ; and execution followed the shout.
Fixing their spears in the ground, in order that they may
be lighter to ascend the steeps, they run upward.   The
Volscians, having discharged their missile weapons at the
first onset, fling the stones lying at their feet on them as
they advanced upward, and, having thrown them into confusion by incessant blows, they drove them from the higher
ground : thus the left wing of the Romans was nearly over-
borne, had not the consul dispelled their fear by exciting a
sense of shame as they were just retreating, chiding at the
same time their temerity and their cowardice.   At first they
stood their ground with determined firmness ; then according as their strength carried them against those in possession
of the ground, they venture to advance themselves ; and,
by renewing the shout, they encourage the whole body to
move on ; then again making a new effort, they force their
way up and surmount the disadvantage of the ground.   They
were on the point of gaining the summit of the eminence,
when the enemy turned their backs, and the pursued and
pursuers with precipitate speed rushed into the camp almost
in a body.   In this consternation the camp is taken ; such

of the Volscians as were able to make their escape take the
road to Antium. The Roman army, also, was led to Antium ; after being invested for a few days, it surrenders
without any additional force of the besiegers,[1] but because
their spirits had sunk ever since the unsuccessful battle and
the loss of their camp.

[1] *Additional force of the*, etc.   Crevier understands this to signify
that the Romans did not employ a greater force for besieging Antium than they had employed the preceding year, and which at that
time seemed insufficient for the purpose. Others understand the
words to signify that they surrendered without waiting for the Romans to make any additional efforts to take the town.

842

CPSIA information can be obtained
at www.ICGtesting.com
Printed in the USA
BVHW040825241120
593995BV00007B/527